CONTE

ACKNOWLEDGMENTS

This book has been an adventure for me. All my friends know I have a fear of writing and so I procrastinate. One day I just sat down at my computer to write words — unfinished thoughts — no sentence structure. Thank you, Marilynn Draxl, for not only putting my thoughts into sentences, but also for being there to encourage me. Thanks to my sister, Ada Jayne Nonn, who was my photographer.

Thanks also to my friends from the Harford Community College Gourd Club who created gourds specifically for this book. I particularly enjoyed the day we got together at Jayne Wright's house and hung out in her barn.

Most of all, I thank all the generous gourd artists who have shared their knowledge and taught me so much over the years through workshops, demonstrations, books, and online gourd groups.

Introduction

IN 1999, WHILE ON A FAMILY VACATION, I attended the Ohio Gourd Society Festival. This was my first introduction to gourds and I was hooked. Not only did I sign up for two workshops with Jayne Stanley, but I also bought five gourds at the festival and a gourd crafting book. Living in Maryland, there was little activity in gourds, i.e., few crafters and no societies. It was through the American Gourd Society's website that I found local gourd growers and tips about crafting gourds. I drove to the closest gourd festivals in North Carolina and Florida for additional workshops and supplies. Twelve years later, I am fortunate to have discovered a craft for which I have a personal passion.

2003 Author's *Fish Tale* gourd with the March/April 2003 *Expression* magazine.

When I started working with gourds, I used my father's tools. If I wanted to cut off the top of a gourd to make a bowl, I used his Black and Decker® jigsaw. It was heavy, but it did the job.

I don't know when I saw the gourd that was painted as a jack-o-lantern in a magazine, but I knew I wanted to make some. I did not paint them; I cut out the face and colored the gourd with orange leather dye. I was still using my father's heavy awkward jigsaw and lots of sandpaper. I remember making over fifty jack-o-lanterns that fall — that was a lot of sanding.

I bought my first mini-jigsaw because of the 2003 March/April issue of *Expression* magazine. Jeanne L. Ames had written an article on how to make fish tale gourds. After three attempts with my father's jigsaw, I bought the Microlux® gourd saw, but I was still unhappy. Yes, I could cut fine lines and tight curves — but I broke the saw blades as fast I replaced them. I remember going through a dozen blades in one afternoon. While many people love the small cup on the mini gourd saw, when I tried to make a turn, I would tilt the saw and break the blade. I remember going back to the Black and Decker jigsaw until I bought the Microlux jigsaw, which has a flatbed that stays perpendicular to the gourd surface so you do not tilt the saw when cutting curves. It is not perfect. It would be difficult to cut concave curves on a Chinese bottle gourd, for example.

Everyone has an opinion on everything, and gourd tools are no exception. I think the best tool for any job is what you have and what you are comfortable with using. I have seen incredible cut-out work by an artist using a rotary tool, wood burner, or just an X-Acto™ knife. I use the flatbed Microlux saw.

Getting Started

Basic Tools

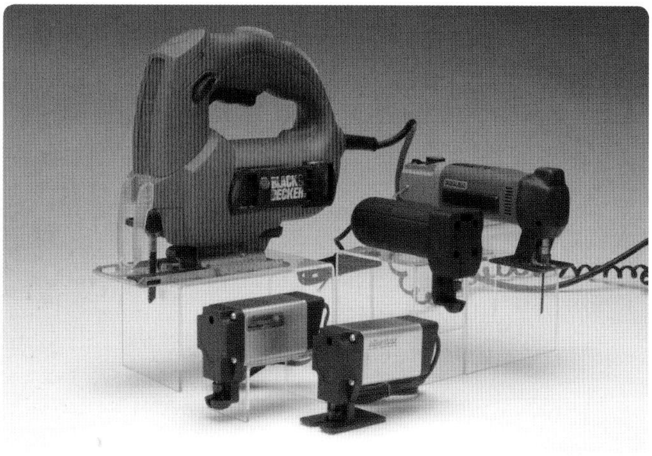

A comparison of jigsaw sizes.

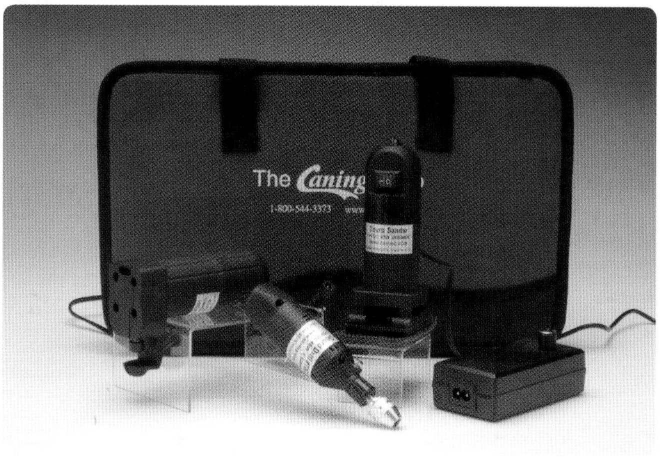

The Caning Shop's Gourd Tool Set includes: the Gourd Saw with 6 blades, the Gourd Drill with an assortment of 6 engraving cutters, the Gourd Sander with 6 sanding sponges, and an 8-18 volt variable speed transformer, all packaged in a soft-sided carrying case.

Saws

Microlux saws are small and light. The flatbed provides stability when cutting. The front of the flatbed reminds me of a sewing machine, providing a guideline for cutting. The blades are thin and extend about half an inch for cutting. People complain that they cannot see the cutting line easily, that the flatbed of the saw is too big. If this is your problem, just cut off part of the flatbed — a suggestion that was made from a member of the online group, "GourdPatch."

I do not think mini-jigsaws are designed to be a work horse, but with care I can cut up to 1/2″-thick gourds. Because I do a lot of cutting, I have two flatbed saws that I rotate between when one saw feels warm in my hand.

Microlux's gourd saw with its small round cup has the advantage of being able to cut curves on some gourds. It also has less of an opening around the saw to see where you are cutting. One of my students cut off half the ball and then painted the remaining ball white to be able to see it better.

Of course, there are other mini-saws, two of which I have not used. I do own the Proxxon® mini-jigsaw and the Gourd Saw® from the Caning Company. I was surprised that these two saws use the same Proxxon blade. The Proxxon saw is awkward to operate without the additional foot pedal. I like the weight and feel of the Gourd Saw for cutting off tops and other simple lines. The blade is too thick for some of the projects in this book. It also vibrates more than the Microlux saws.

One of the things that I like about the Caning Company's saw is that it can come bundled with a carver and sander. The bundle includes their transformer and converters that you can connect to a Proxxon transformer. For someone who has not already invested in a variety of tools, this is a nice combination.

Blades

The Microlux saw uses three different blades: fine, coarse, and diamond. The difference between fine and coarse is the number of teeth per inch on the blade. There are more teeth on the fine blade than on the coarse blade. I use the coarse blade on my gourd projects. I try to use at least .25-inch thick gourds for my projects, the exception being cannonball gourds. Cannonball gourds (here on the East Coast) tend to be thinner but denser. The coarse blade holds up under the thicker and/or denser gourds.

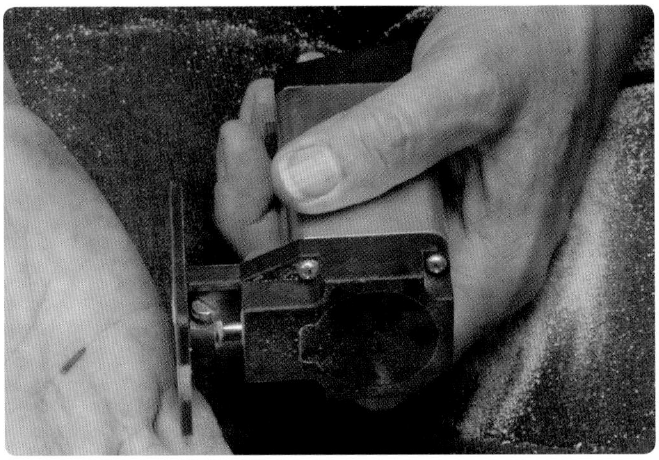

Changing blades on a Microlux® jigsaw.

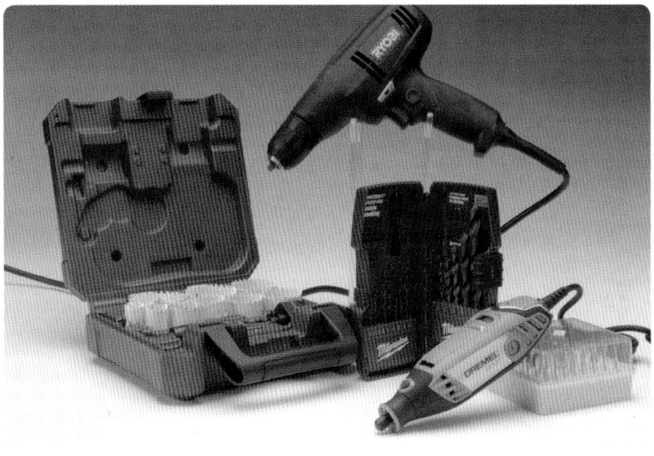

Additional basic tools for gourd crafting .

The diamond blade is interesting in that you can cut both forward and backward. For me, the best use of the diamond blade is to smooth cuts you have already made.

No matter what saw you use, you are going to break blades, so get comfortable replacing them. Often you'll break the blade at the edge of the saw so no part of the blade is visible. I found the easiest way to remove the portion of the broken blade inside the saw is to first lightly loosen the screw on the side of the saw and then turn the saw on to shoot the loose portion of the blade into your hand. To replace the new blade, you might have to loosen the screw a little more. The blade should go in smoothly; then retighten the screw.

Other Tools

For the projects in this book and for most basic gourd crafting, there are other tools that are just as important as a saw, such as a drill with assorted bits, a rotary tool with burs, and sanders.

A drill saves time. It is convenient for making starting holes for your saw. I have cleaning balls and sanding disks that attach to my drill, and this year I treated myself to a set of hole saw bits with a separate quick change arbor. I also use a wide range of regular drill bits — from 1/16 to 1/2 inch. I have a drill with a cord that never runs down, works forever. I have seen students using battery-pack drills in classes. These are heavier and sometimes lose power.

Another important tool is a carving or rotary tool. The most common is the Dremel® brand with a wide variety of accessories. I own several Dremels, a Wecheer®, and a Fordom®. I use my Dremel most of the time because it is convenient and I am comfortable with its weight.

Because I am left-handed, I cannot use the Flexi-shaft attachment that you can buy for a Dremel. The Flexi-shaft allows you to hold a much lighter rotary head piece while the Dremel motor is suspended above. After breaking three Flexi-shafts, I was told that because I am left-handed, I force the coil in the shaft to twist and eventually break. If you are right-handed and have a Dremel, I would recommend the Flexi-shaft.

There are catalogs of burs for any of the rotary tools. The first resource that made sense to me was Bonnie Gibson's Arizona Gourd website (www.arizonagourds.com) because she has taken the time to explain the differences among the burs.

Basic Tools

Inks, dyes, paints, and sprays for coloring gourds.

The last tool I want to mention is not a power tool, but a set of metal rings. They help me create a level line on my gourd when I want to cut the tops off. They are inexpensive and very convenient.

Color and Sealers

You could write books about how to color a gourd — and many have been written. There are dyes, inks, waxes, and paints available. The first class I taught at the Gourd Gathering was titled "The Color Red Twenty Different Ways."

No matter how you color your gourd, inside and/or out, make sure the surface is well prepared. For most gourds, I check to make sure the hard white wax is removed. Some gourds I sand for that polished look.

I do not have a favorite coloring method for the outside of a gourd. I have a tendency to combine color techniques. For example, if I use leather dye on a gourd and do not like the way the gourd absorbed the dye, I will enhance it with Design Master® sprays, Adirondack® inks, or Gilders Paste®. I think Gilders Paste has saved many a gourd.

When it comes to sealing a gourd, what I use depends on how I colored the gourd. I like the look of Briwax® and how the gourd absorbs the wax. Buffing gives it a soft glow, but I cannot use Briwax if I want to keep a mottled pattern (created by either small drops of dyes that have been spritzed with alcohol or inks that have been stamped).

Waxes, rub-ons, and sprays for sealing gourds.

The Briwax will remove excess dyes or inks and blend the colors together. I have learned that the hard way.

Deft® is a clear lacquer spray in satin, semi-gloss, or gloss. It dries fast and leaves a smooth feel. Another spray I would like to mention is Helmsman® Spar Urethane. Not only does it protect finishes from moisture, but also from ultraviolet rays.

There are shelves of sealers, e.g., sprays, wipe-ons, and paint-ons, in hardware stores. I have only mentioned the ones I use.

SAFETY

DUST, MOLD, CHEMICALS, AND CARELESSNESS

Sometimes, the things we love to do carry a health hazard. While I am not talking about the kinds of hazards that come with bungee jumping or rappelling down a mountain, the fact is that a sedentary craft such as gourd-making can have health-related issues.

When a gourd dries, it loses approximately ninety percent of its weight. As the moisture evaporates through the gourd skin, it produces mold. I have noticed there are big differences between the mold on Pennsylvania gourds and Arizona gourds. Pennsylvania gourds have a soft black mold with a small amount of white wax mold. The black mold is easily removed with a copper scrubbie. The white wax simply requires additional scrubbing. Arizona gourds are covered with mostly a hard white wax mold that is difficult to remove.

Every craft, hobby, or activity has risks, and gourds are no exception. Paying attention and using common sense is my best advice for staying whole and healthy.

To safely remove mold, my Gourd Patch friends have recommended:

- Burying them in potting soil
- Soaking in fabric softener
- Filling a black plastic leaf bag with water and gourds and letting them warm up in the sun.

All of these suggestions work. If you buy gourds with mold on the outside, consider a wet method. It helps eliminate inhaling gourd mold when cleaning the outside surface. A lot of gourd growers now clean their gourds, which eliminates this step.

I also clean the inside of my gourds with water. After cutting off the top or cutting a hole, I fill the gourd with water and let it soak for two to three days. I use a canning jar lid to scrap the gourd pulp out. It is another way to reduce breathing in mold and dust.

If you choose to sand your gourds or use one of the cleaning balls, you will produce a lot of gourd dust. Please use a respiratory system or dust collector when sanding or grinding. I do all of my cleaning, sanding, and grinding outside. In the summer, I use three box fans to keep the gourd dust away.

Also be aware of chemicals in your dyes and sealers. Always work in a well-ventilated area, preferably outside.

The last safety thing I want to mention is care around the use of power tools as these can be hazardous to your health. I have seen a student drill a hole in her hand. Another student got her long hair caught in the drill. Don't wear loose clothes, tie back long hair, sit down when using tools, and pay attention to what you are doing. Don't be distracted, especially in a class or workshop environment. Take care of yourself.

Projects

ALL THE PROJECTS IN THIS BOOK WERE DONE with the MicroLux flatbed mini-jigsaw, but they could also have been done with other tools. The purpose of this book is not to promote specific products. If you don't have a mini-jigsaw, use what you have and what you are comfortable with.

As well as a cutting tool, you will need a drill, bits, and a rotary tool with various burs. At the beginning of each project is a material list of specific things that are mentioned in the instructions.

These are simple projects to get you comfortable with your mini-jigsaw. As you improve your skills, consider trying to add depth to the projects by wood-burning more details and shadows into them or creating a more three-dimensional look with carving. This is just a stepping-off point. Most of all, though, have fun!

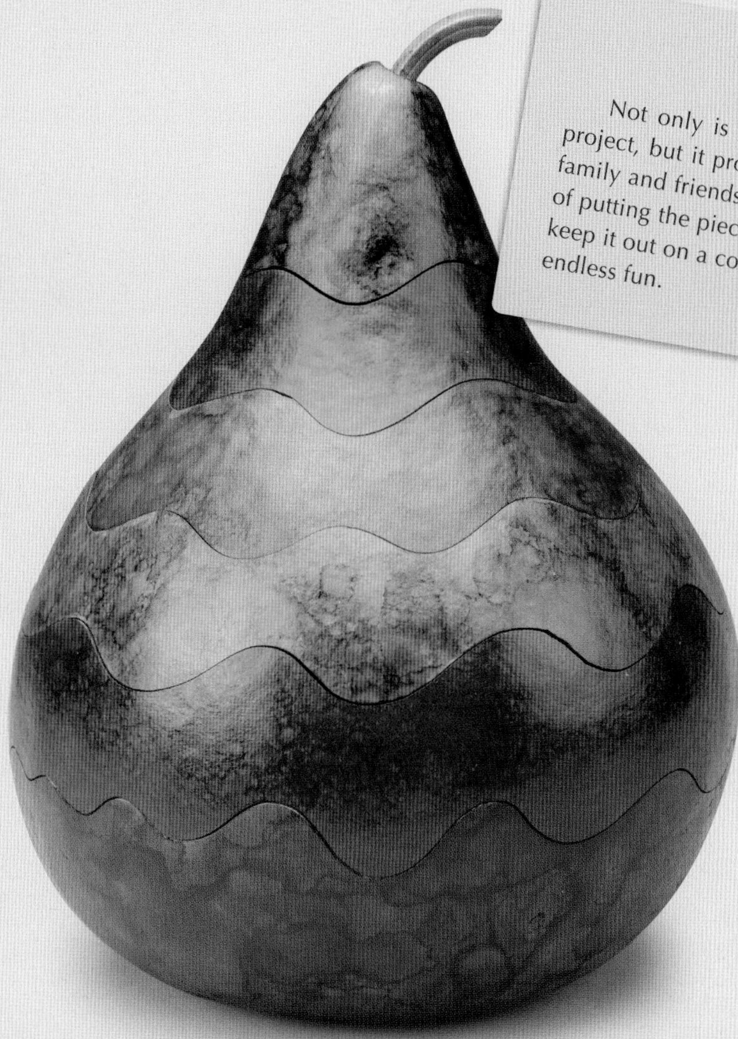

Puzzles

Not only is creating a gourd puzzle a fun project, but it provides hours of amusement for family and friends who step-up to the challenge of putting the pieces in place. I suggest that you keep it out on a coffee table for easy access and endless fun.

Puzzle Ring

If you just acquired your first saw, this is a great beginner's project with its gentle curves. You don't have to be that accurate. If you accidentally go off the line, you can just gently move back on course. The most important thing is to end exactly where you started. After cutting the rings, the fun is in the coloring. I chose to use Adirondack inks, but you could use paint, wax, or go natural. See page 87 for other examples of finishes for this project.

Multi-ring puzzle stamped with Adirondack inks.

Materials needed:

- X-Acto knife (I use a #2)
- Acrylic paint
- Clear drying glue
- Adirondack inks
- Adirondack alcohol ink applicator
- Clear sealer

What You Do:

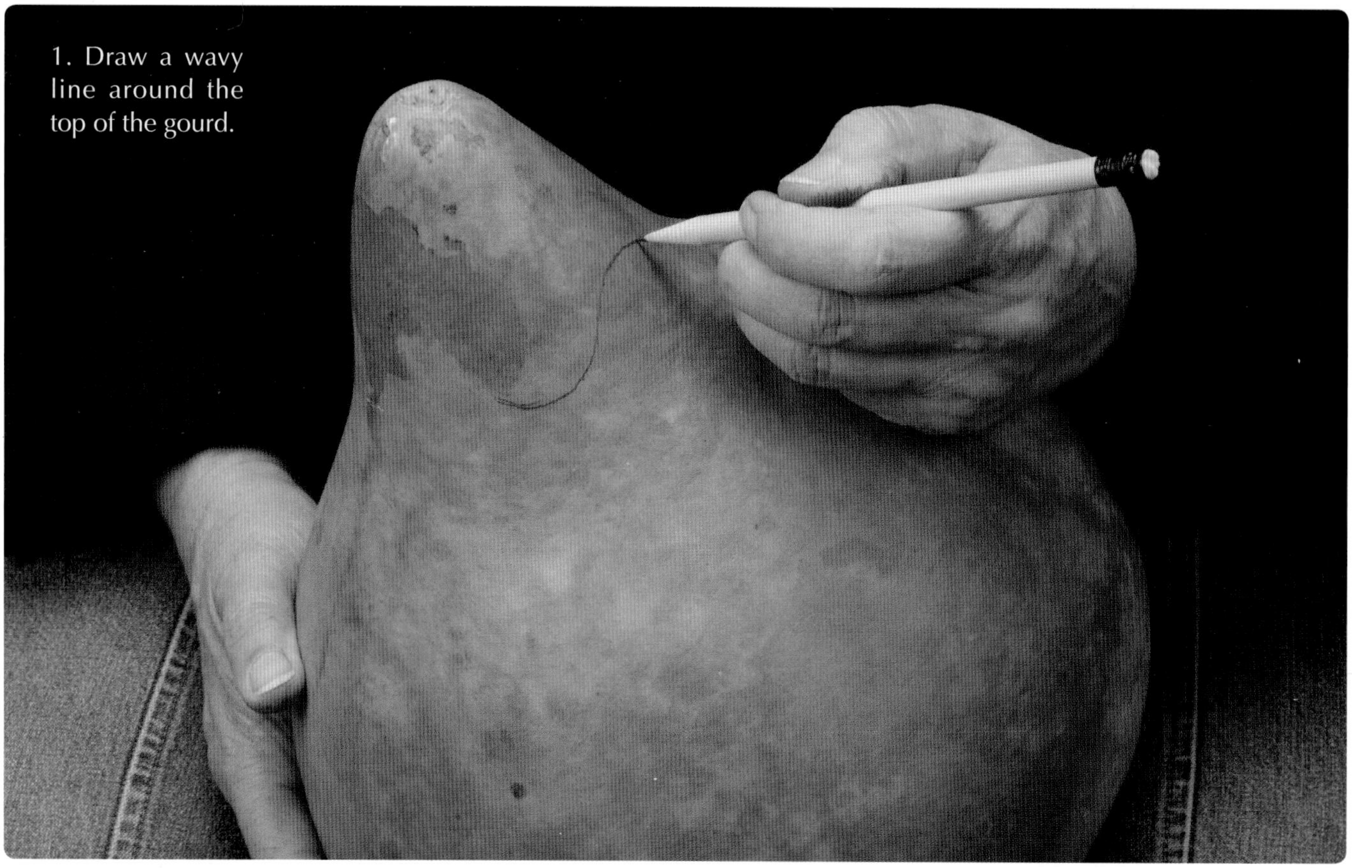

1. Draw a wavy line around the top of the gourd.

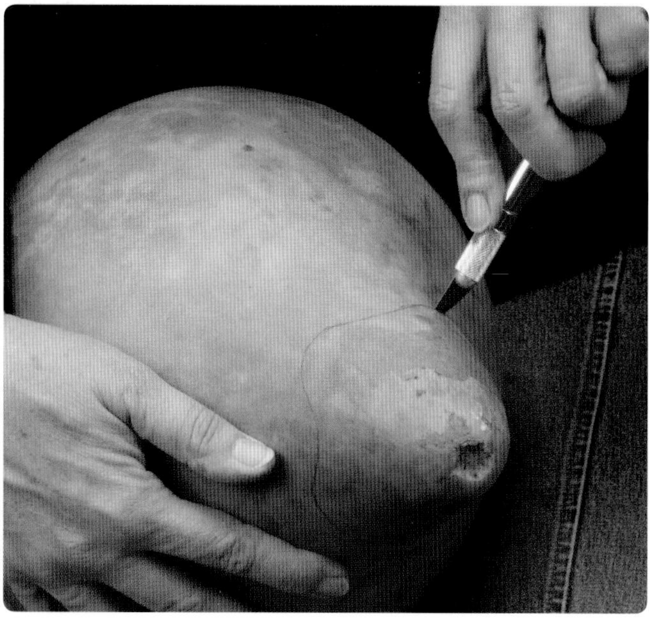

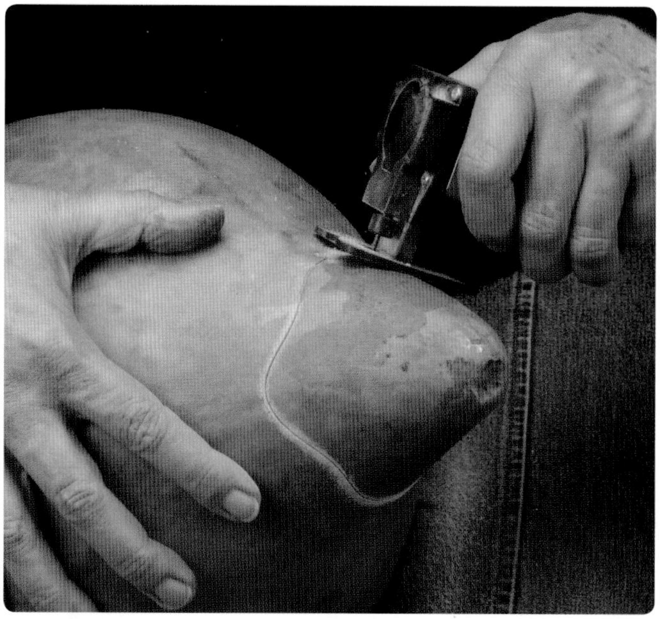

2. Using an X-Acto knife, create a slit to insert the mini-jigsaw's blade. I usually try to find the longest straight edge of my curvy line.

3. Insert the mini-jigsaw blade and try to follow your line.

4. Repeat steps one through three to create a series of stacking rings. Never go below the widest circumference of the gourd to leave a bowl shape bottom to the puzzle.

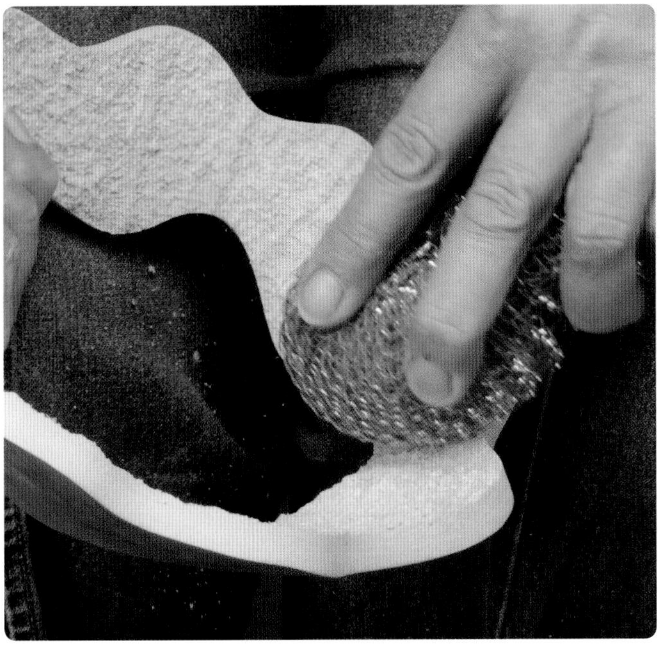

5. Depending on the amount of pulp, clean the inside of the rings with a steel scrubbie. If there is a lot of pulp, scrape first with either an X-Acto knife or your favorite gourd scraper.

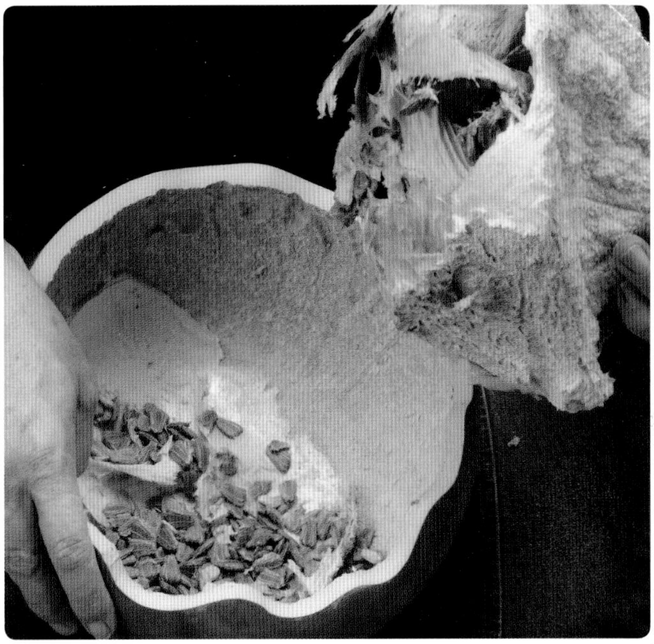

6. On the bottom of the bowl, pull out any loose pulp.

7. Use a concrete ball to grind away any difficult pulp. Afterwards, smooth with the steel scrubbie.

8. Paint the inside and the edges of the puzzle with a half-and-half combination of acrylic paint and Elmer's glue. The glue helps the paint adhere to the textured surface.

9. Place three to four drops of Adirondack Ink on the edge of the applicator.

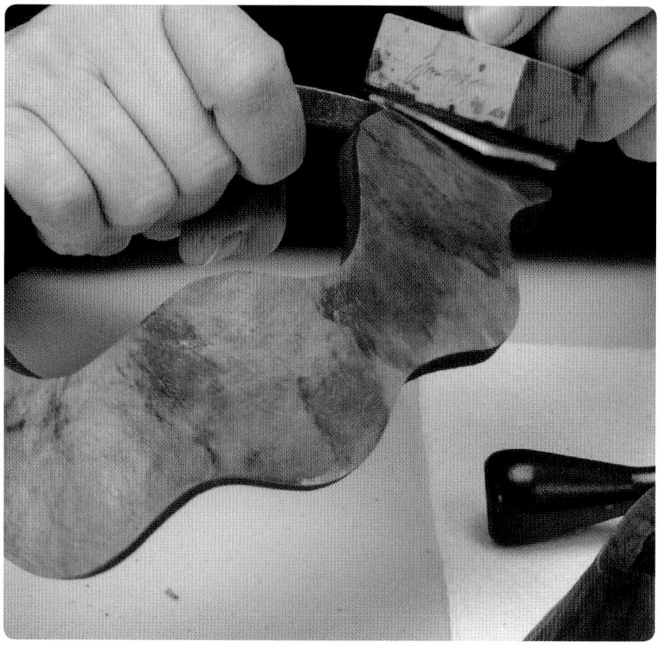

10. Stamp color on the outside of the gourd ring. If you rub, you will get a smooth color. If you stamp (pound on the gourd), you will create a texture.
11. Spray with a clear finish, such as Deft semi-gloss.

12. This gourd was missing a stem, so I drilled a hole and attached a new stem (make sure you color the stem).

13. Assemble the puzzle rings after they have dried.

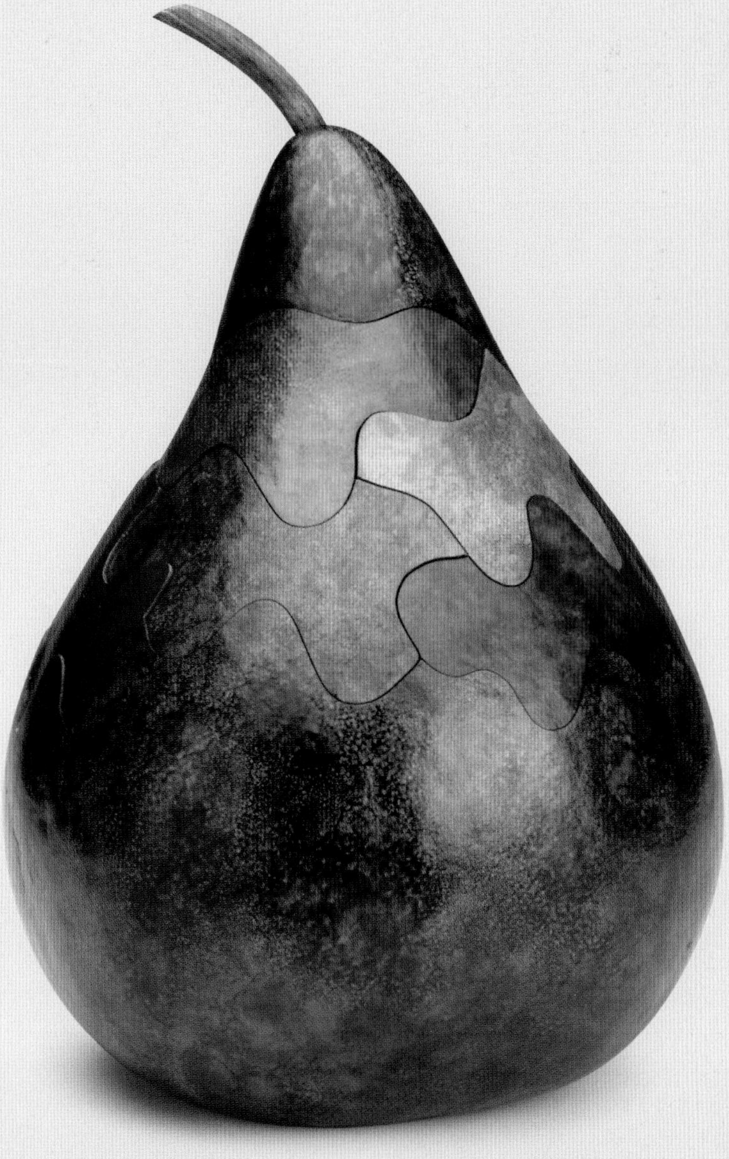

PUZZLE PIECES

In this project, instead of rings, you will cut the gourd up in sections.
Here are some rules or guidelines to ensure the puzzle can be easily assembled and won't collapse:

Multi-piece puzzle gourd stamped with Adirondack inks.

- Never go below the widest circumference of the gourd.
- The structure support of the gourd is based on the roman arch principal.
- Your curves should be wider at the top than the bottom.
- It is better to cut vertical tall pieces than wide ones.

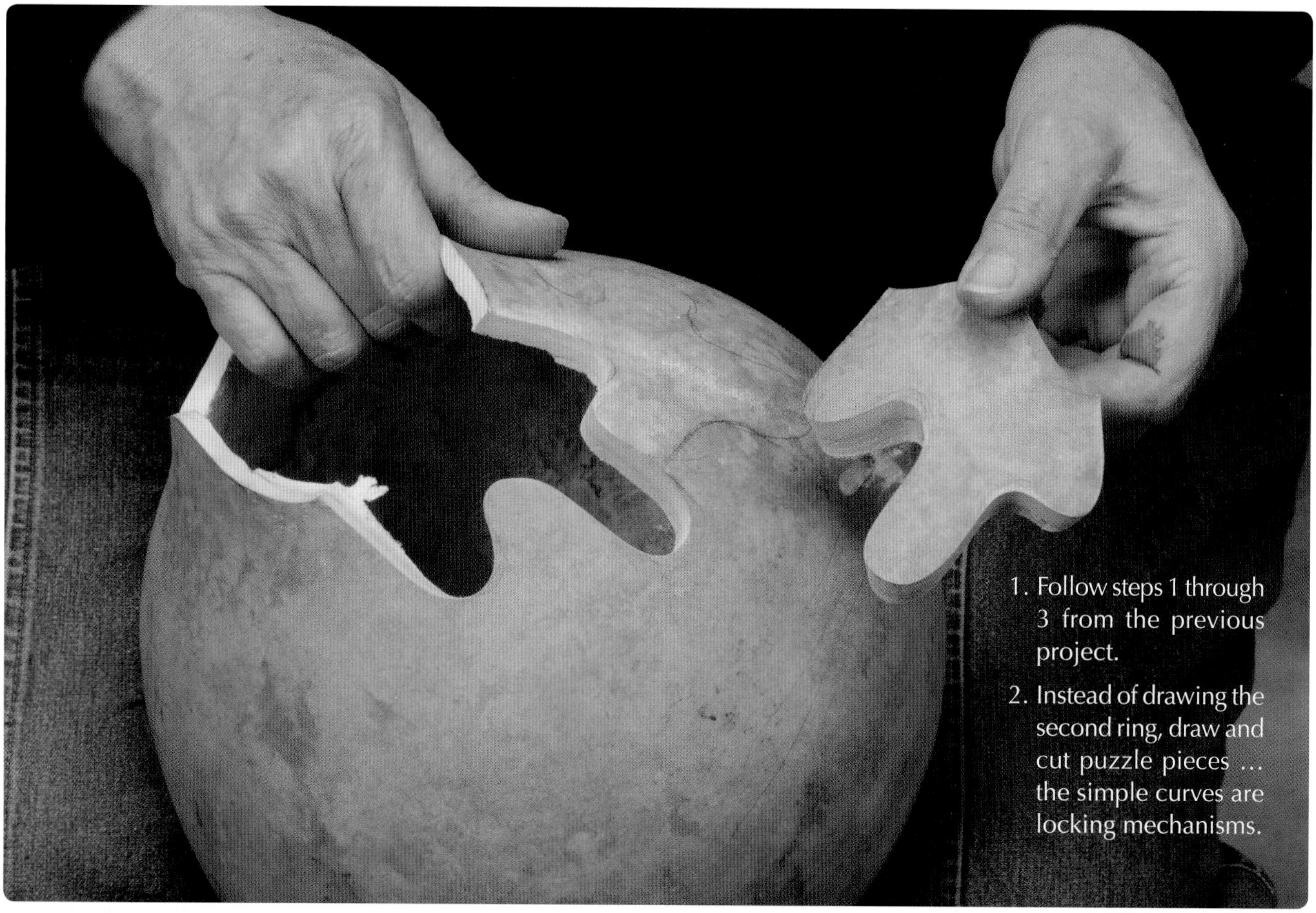

1. Follow steps 1 through 3 from the previous project.
2. Instead of drawing the second ring, draw and cut puzzle pieces ... the simple curves are locking mechanisms.

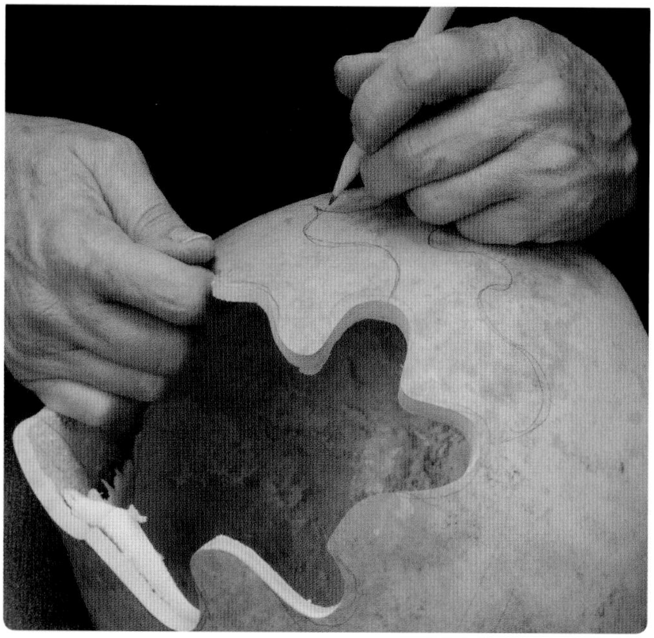

3. Don't go beyond the widest point of the gourd.

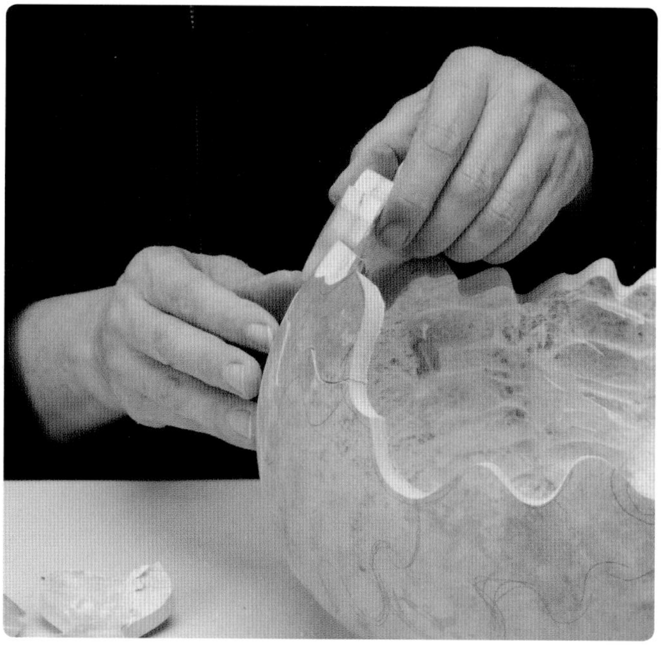

4. Finish the puzzle by following steps five through twelve.

Saw Doodles

I have always admired filigree work done on a gourd. My favorite is Bob Dillard's cannon ball gourd. When I try to cut with such precision, though, I am often in despair, not because of my cutting, but because of my inability to draw the design accurately. In the end, my filigree looks more like doodling than precision cuts, but it is fun nonetheless. If you appreciate the latest craze in Zen Doodling, you will enjoy learning to Saw Doodle.

Robert Dillard's spiral-cut designs. *From the author's collection.*

Materials needed:

- Acrylic paint
- Clear drying glue
- Red Leather dye
- Cranberry Design master spray
- Sealer

What You Do:

1. Draw a wiggly line around the very top of the gourd.
2. Drill a hole and cut off the top.
3. Clean the inside of the gourd with your favorite cleaning tools.
4. Paint the inside of the gourd with a combination of acrylic paint and clear drying glue.

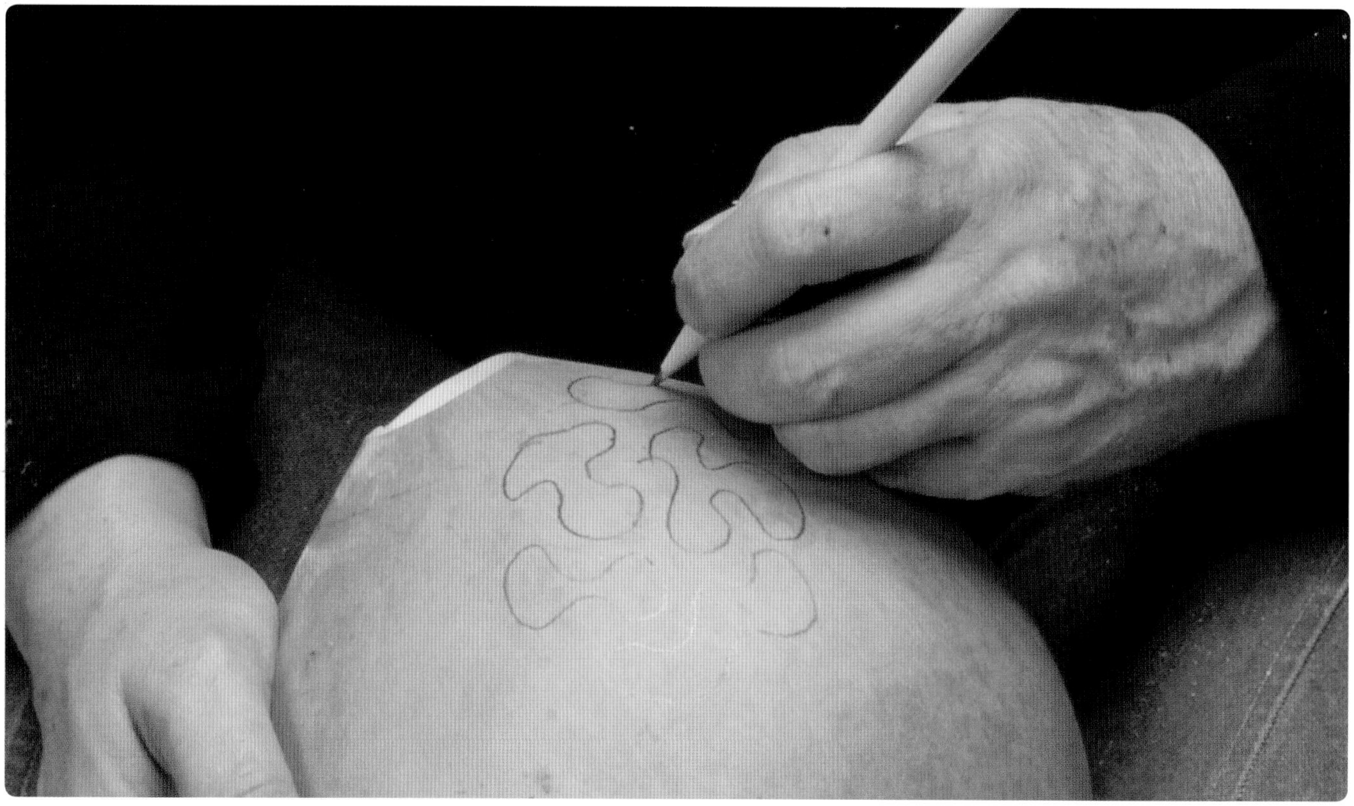

5. Draw "amoebas" on the gourd, i.e., single-cell organisms you see under the microscope — little wiggly shapes. Keep an even space between your "amoebas."
6. Drill a hole in each "amoeba."

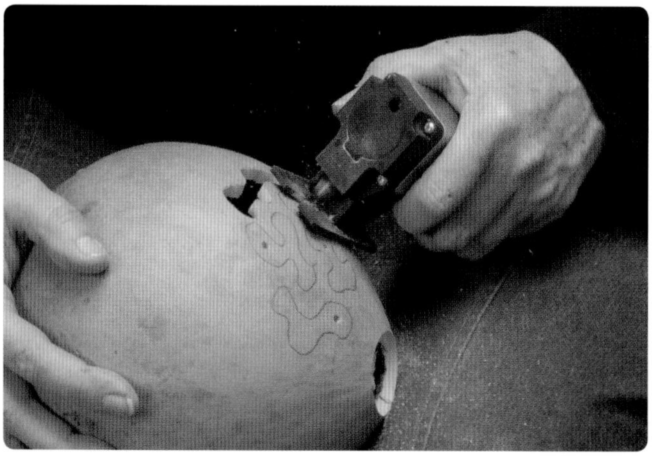

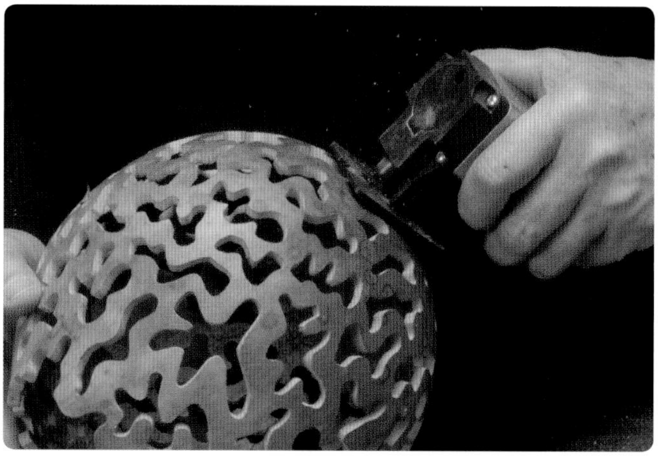

7. Cut out the wiggly shapes. *(**If you're comfortable enough, you can skip Step 5. Just drill holes and cut the "amoebas.")*

8. If necessary, use a rotary tool with a sanding bit to smooth any edges.
9. Clean out the gourd dust with a hair dryer or leaf blower.

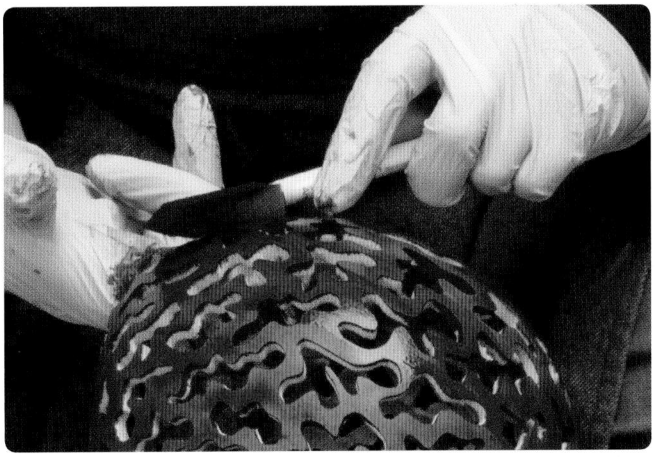

10. Dye or paint the outside of the gourd and cut out edges.
11. Seal with a lacquer spray.

THE FOLLOWING PIECES WERE DONE BY SOME OF MY GOURD FRIENDS SPECIFICALLY FOR THIS BOOK.

Doodling on a Saturday afternoon.

Raku waxed doodling. *Courtesy of Jayne Wright.*

Christmas Bells. *Courtesy of Jayne Wright.*

Maranka Doodle. *Courtesy of JoAnne Phelps.*

CIRCLE DESIGN WITH GINKGO LEAVES

I fell in love with Susan Zanella's autumn circle design and asked if I could include it as a project. Using the simplicity of a circle, the possibilities of design ideas are endless. The instructions are for ginkgo leaves. The graceful curves of the leaves are easy to cut.

Circle Cut-Out Oak Leaves.
Courtesy of Susan M. Zanella.

Materials needed:

- Compass
- Black Acrylic Paint
- Clear Drying Glue
- Brown and Green Leather Dye
- Clear Briwax
- African Bronze and Inca Gold Gilders Paste

1. Draw a wavy line around the top of the gourd.
2. Using an X-Acto knife, create a slit to insert the mini-jigsaw's blade. Try to find the longest straight edge of your curvy line
3. Insert the mini-jigsaw blade and cut off the top of the gourd (the same way you created the first ring in the puzzle gourd project).
4. Remove all the inside pulp with your favorite cleaning tools.

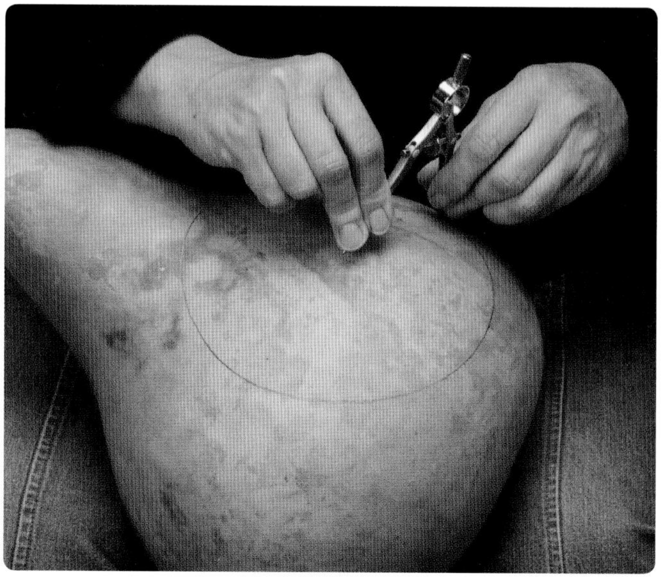

5. Using a compass, draw the largest circle on the side of a martin gourd. Leave approximately two inches between the edge of the circle and the top of the gourd.

6. Use the gingko leaf pattern to draw a design that flows through the circle. If you want to see your completed design in advance, tape all of your leaf patterns on the gourd using double-sided tape. At the end of this project, you will find an example of a leaf arrangement.
7. Inside the circle, drill holes in the areas that will be cut out.

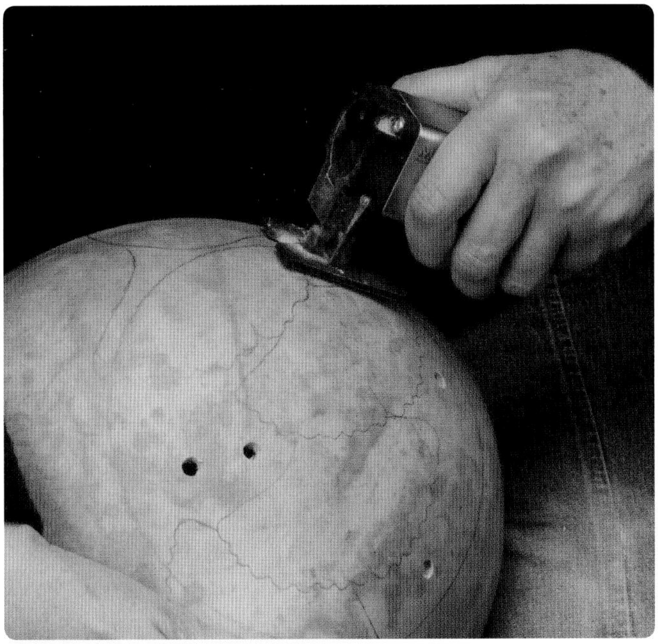

8. Insert saw blade to cut out the inside sections of the circle. Remember to keep your saw flat on the gourd surface.

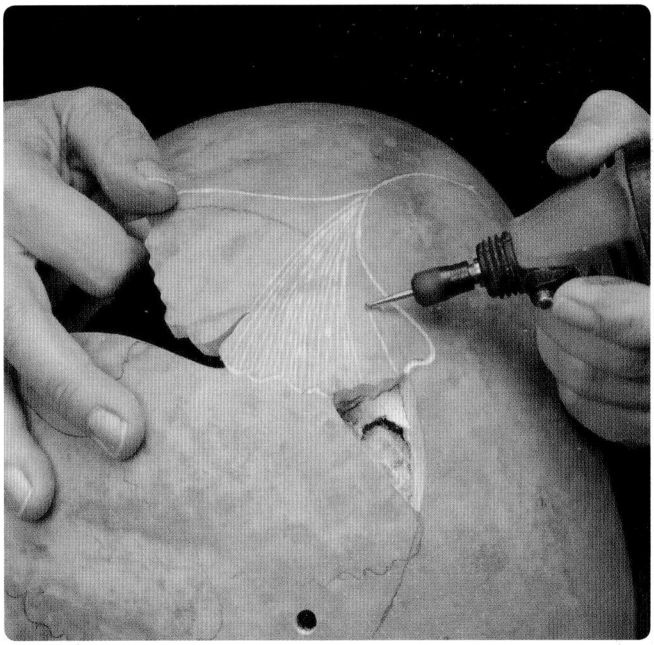

9. To highlight the gingkos, use a rotary carving tool and a ball bit to carve veins. And carve any outside edges of the leaves.

10. Check inside of gourd for any "pulp" not removed in beginning.

11. Use sandpaper to smooth any rough area.

12. Paint inside of lid and gourd with a combination of black acrylic paint and clear drying glue.

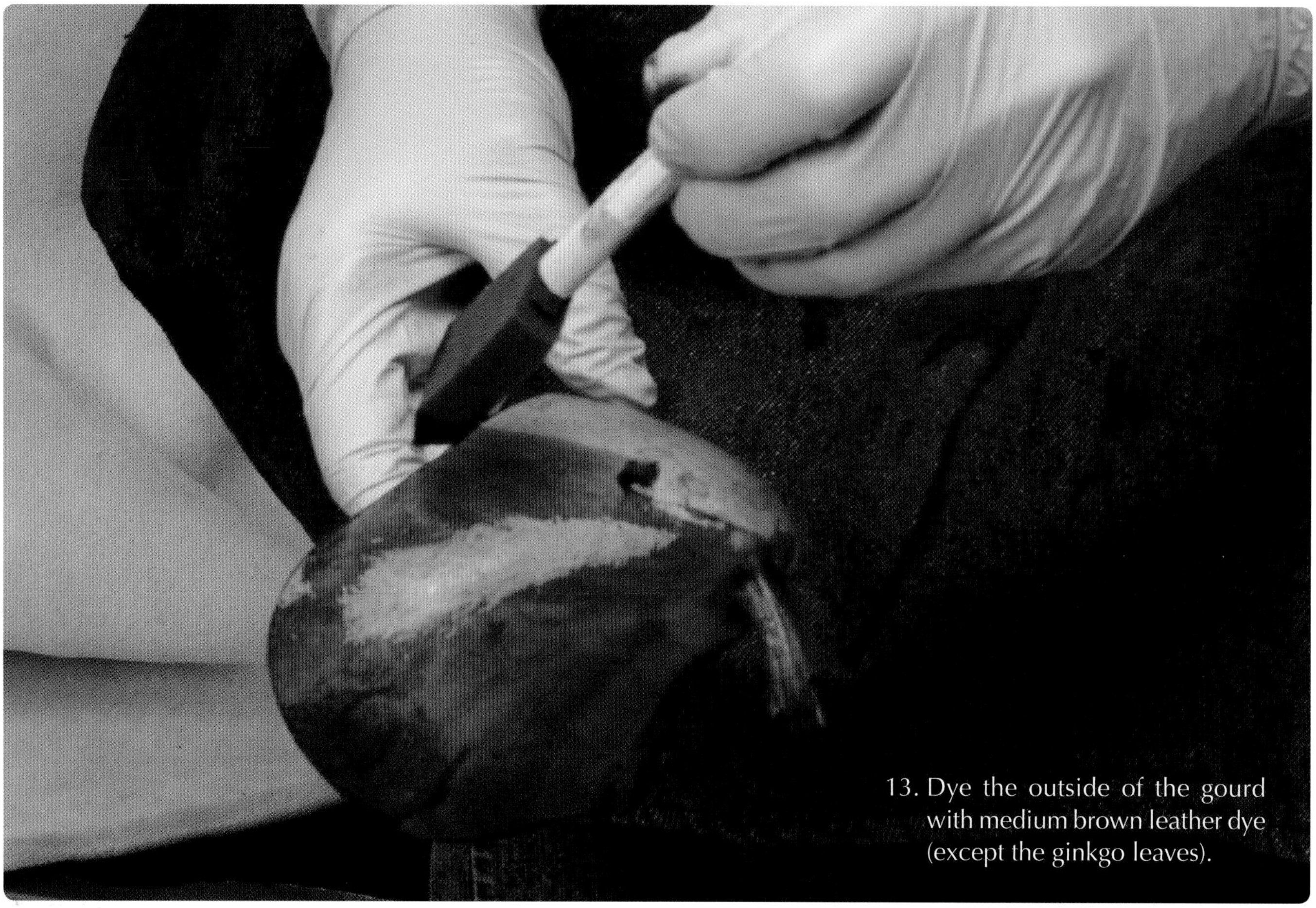

13. Dye the outside of the gourd with medium brown leather dye (except the ginkgo leaves).

14. Dye ginkgo leaves green.

15. Wipe on Briwax; wait three minutes and buff.

16. Cover ginkgo leaves with African Bronze gilder's paste. In small areas, use the tips of your fingers to apply gilder's paste. For larger areas, use a stiff brush. If you color off the ginkgo leaf onto the brown dye, you can remove the unwanted color with a pencil eraser.

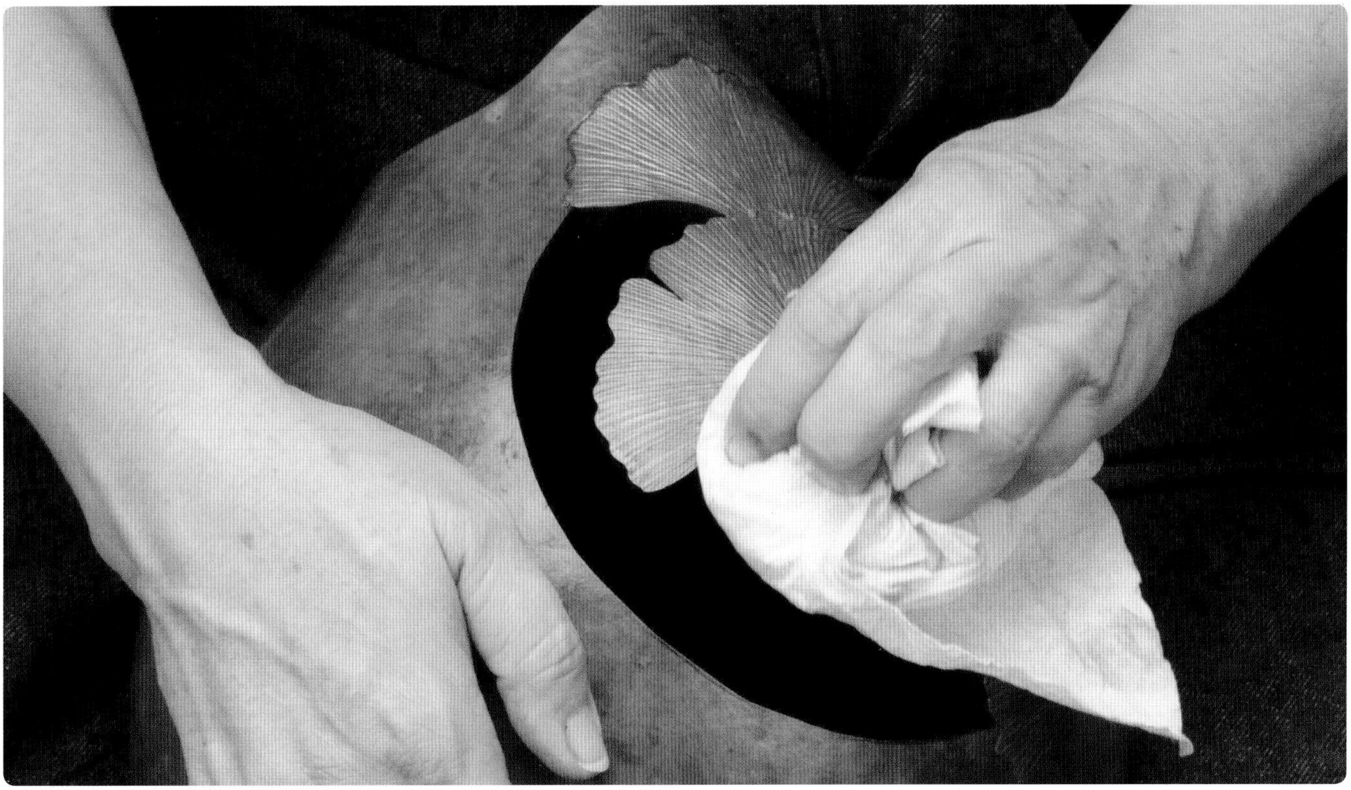

17. Buff the ginkgo area to a sheen. Gilder's Paste not only colors, but seals.
18. Optional: Highlight your leaves with Inca Gold and then buff again.

Paper pattern of Ginkgo leaves.

Finished circle cut-out with Ginkgo leaves.

The circle cut-out design works with so many shapes.
Here are some additional ideas.

Tropical Foliage. *Courtesy of JoAnne Phelps*.

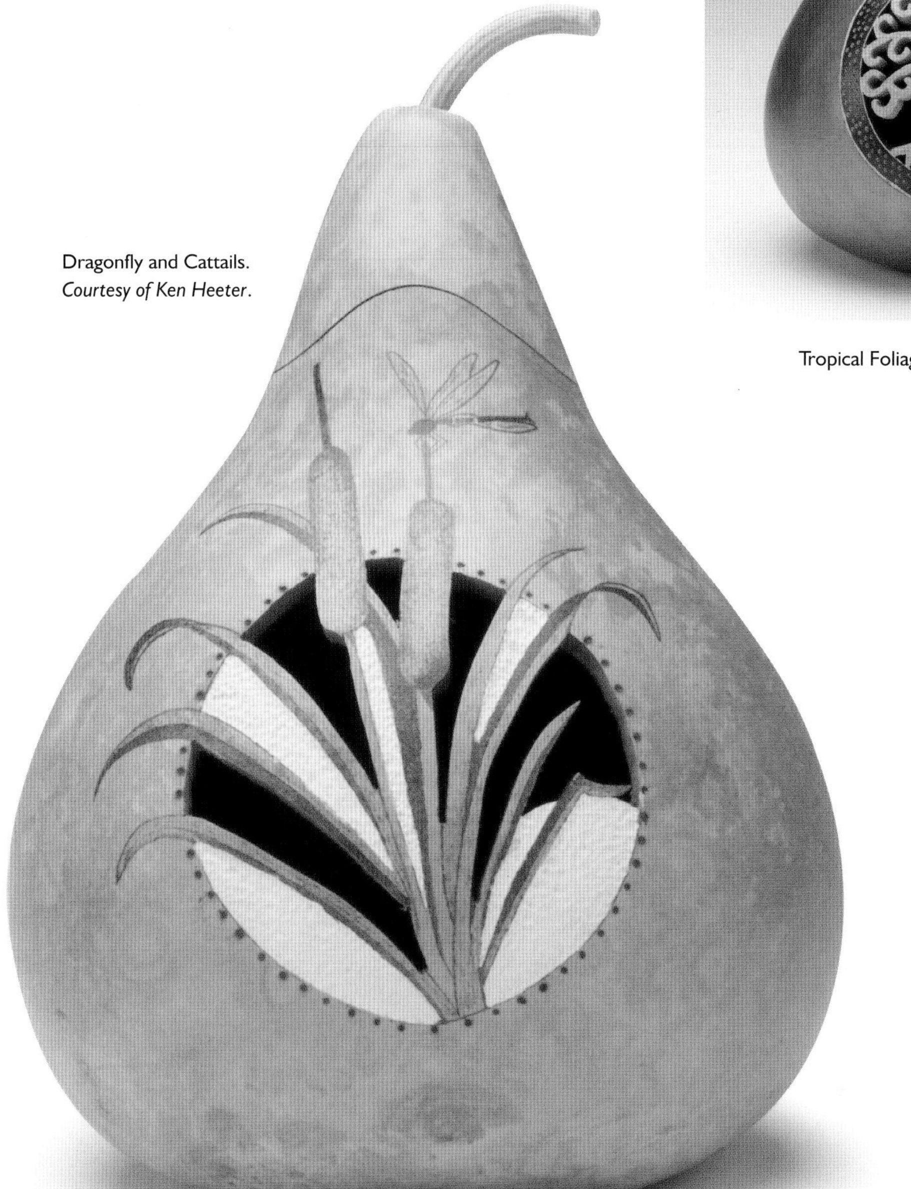

Dragonfly and Cattails.
Courtesy of Ken Heeter.

Circling Trout. *Courtesy of Susan M. Zanella*.

Tropical Foliage. *Courtesy of Susan M. Zanella*.

Wreath Exercise

I was looking for inexpensive class projects (under $10) and thought of cutting out individual leaves to attach to a ready-made twig wreath. I bought a large cracked gourd for $2 and was able to create fourteen oak leaves of various sizes. Once I cut out the leaves, the ideas for their use were endless. I have included some additional leaf photos to inspire you.

Materials needed:

- Cracked or misshapen gourds
- 15/32″ size eye screws
- Florist or rusty wire
- Twig wreath
- Optional embellishments (ribbons and bows, natural botanicals, felted acorns)
- Stampin' Up® Inks
- Q-Tips
- Brown acrylic paint
- Clear drying glue

Twig wreath with cut out gord leaves colored with Stampin' Up inks.

What You Do:

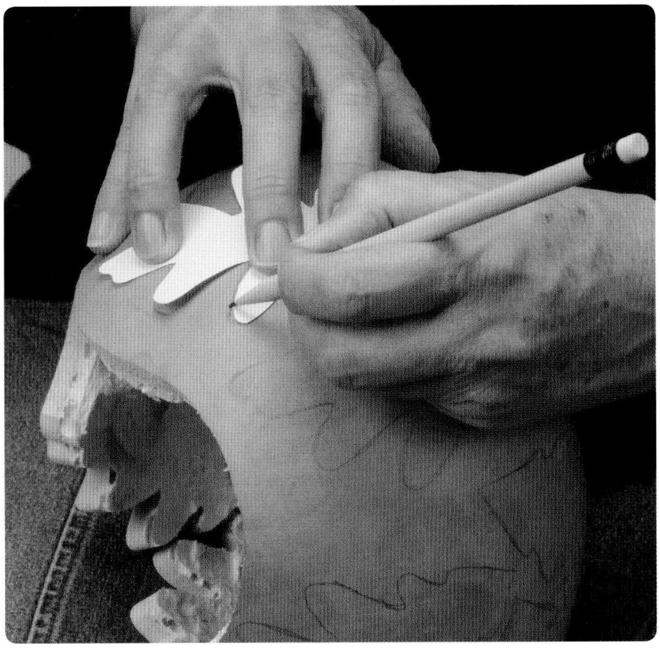

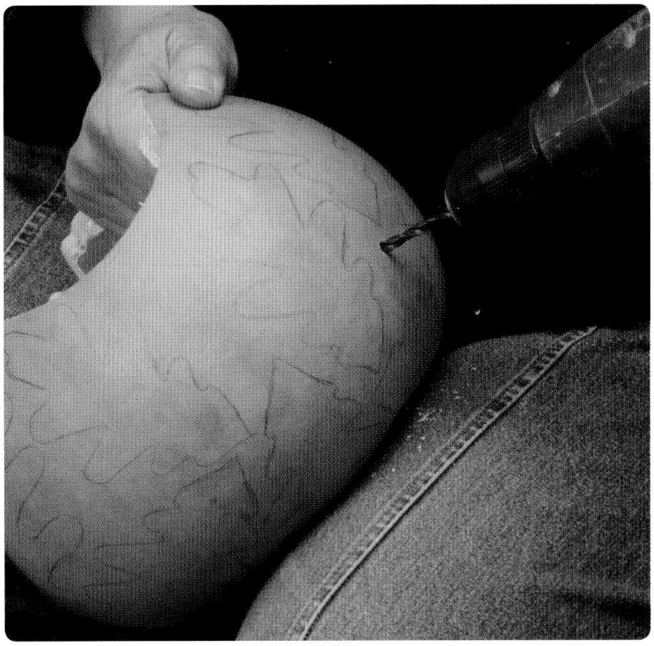

1. Trace your favorite leaf design all over the cracked or misshapen gourd. I recommend the white oak leaf with rounded leaf lobes because it's easier to start with than the sharp points of a red oak leaf. On *page 40,* there are leaf patterns for you to try.

2. Drill a small hole, large enough to insert the saw blade. The MicroLux blade can fit into a 1/16″ drilled hole.

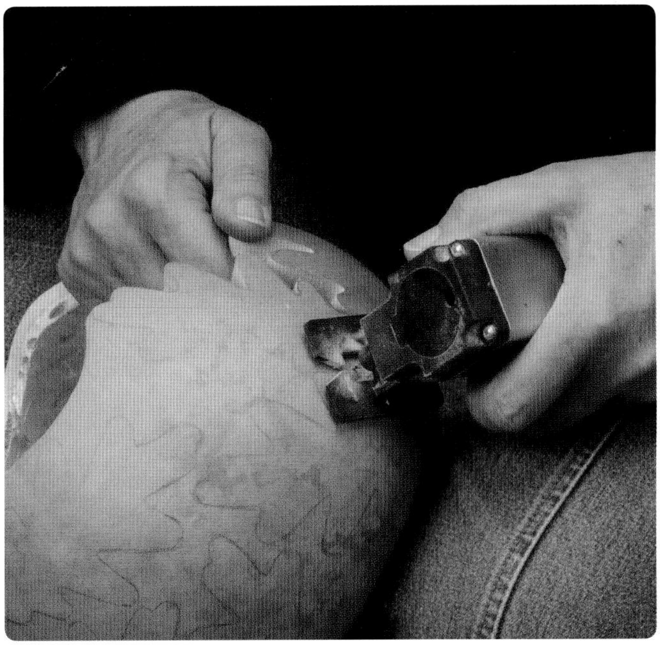

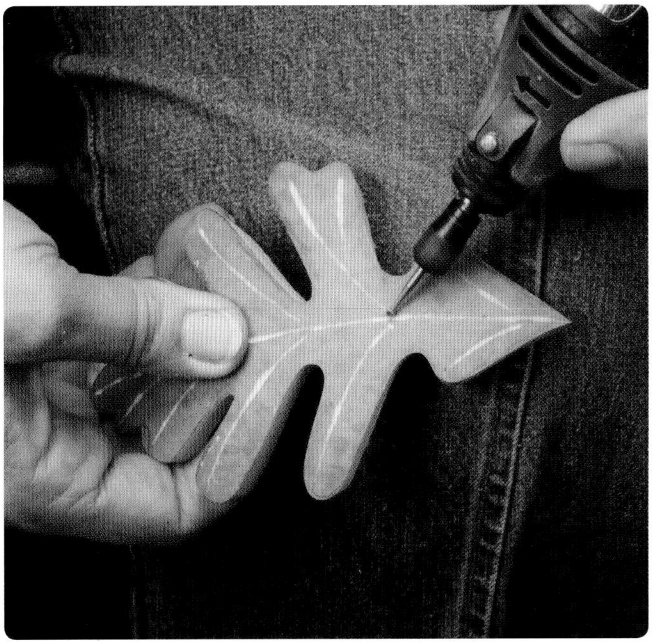

3. Cut out the interior curves in one movement. Remember to stay relaxed, guide the blade, do not push the saw.

4. Practice your smooth curves as you cut out the remaining leaves.

5. To enhance the look of the leaves, carve veins using a ball bit and a rotary tool.

6. Clean the backside of the gourd. The gourd pulp can be scraped off with an X-Acto knife or kitchen paring knife. If it is difficult to remove the pulp, soak the back of the leaves in a dish of warm water for 15 to 20 minutes and the pulp should easily pull off.

7. Scour the back with a copper scouring pad or use medium-grade sandpaper to smooth the surface.

8. Paint the back of the leaf with a half-and-half mixture of brown acrylic paint and clear glue.
9. Color the edges of the leaf with brown leather dye.

10. Using Q-tips, color the leaves with Stampin' Up Craft Inks. Blend the colors by slightly rubbing one color into another with your fingers.
11. Seal with Deft lacquer semi-gloss.

12. Arrange leaves on a twig wreath.

13. Attach "15/32" screw eyes and 6 inches of florist wire or rusty wire.

14. Attach leaves to wreath by dropping two wires through the twigs and twisting tightly underneath.

15. If you want, you can add bows or other enhancements. I decorated my wreath with felted acorns and a bow.

When cutting out your leaves, how many blades did you break? More importantly, did you stop and figure out why they broke, i.e., did you push or tilt the saw? Did you remove the new blade while it was still running? Was the saw overheating? If you realize why your blade broke, you can improve your technique in the future.

Other Ideas for Cut-Out Leaves

Create a door decoration.

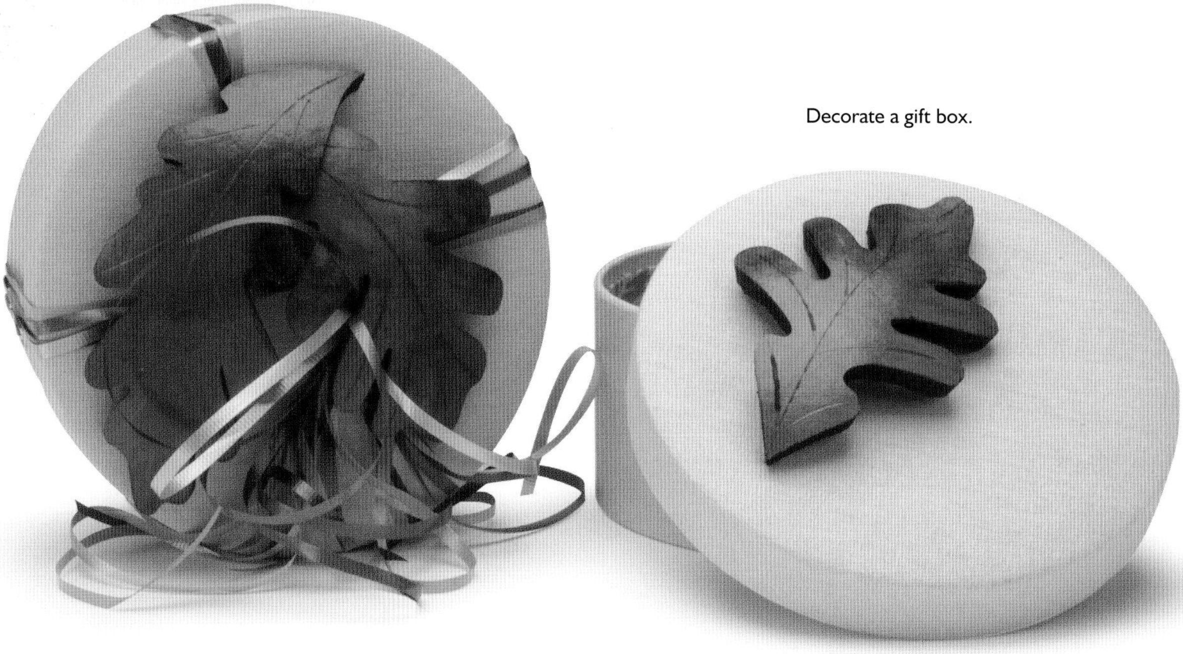
Decorate a gift box.

Attach leaves to auction finds.

Attach leaves to a gourd.

Enhance a basket.

Leaf Bowls

An earlier project involved cutting out leaves to improve your ability to cut curves with your saw. Once you are comfortable with cutting curves, you can overlap your leaves to create a bowl or vase.

Leaf Bowl

Finished leaf bowl.

Materials needed:

- Brown, Yellow, Green, Orange, and Red Leather dyes
- African Bronze, Inca Gold, and Verdigris Gilder's Paste
- Metallic Antique Copper Acrylic Paint
- Clear Drying Glue

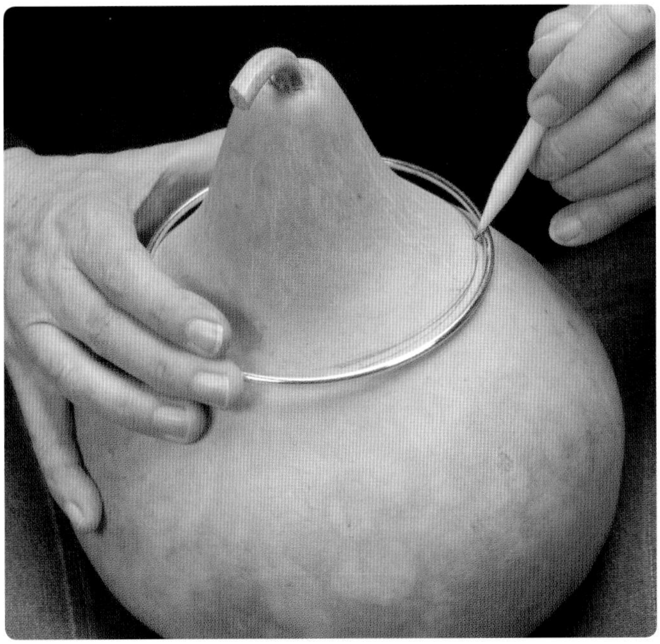

1. Draw a line and cut off the top of the gourd. You can use a set of metal rings to create a top that is parallel to the bottom of the gourd.
2. Clean inside of gourd.
3. Paint the inside of the gourd with half-and-half acrylic metallic antique copper and clear drying glue.
4. Using the leaf pattern *(on following pages)*, trace leaves over the entire gourd making sure you overlap the leaves in at least two places.

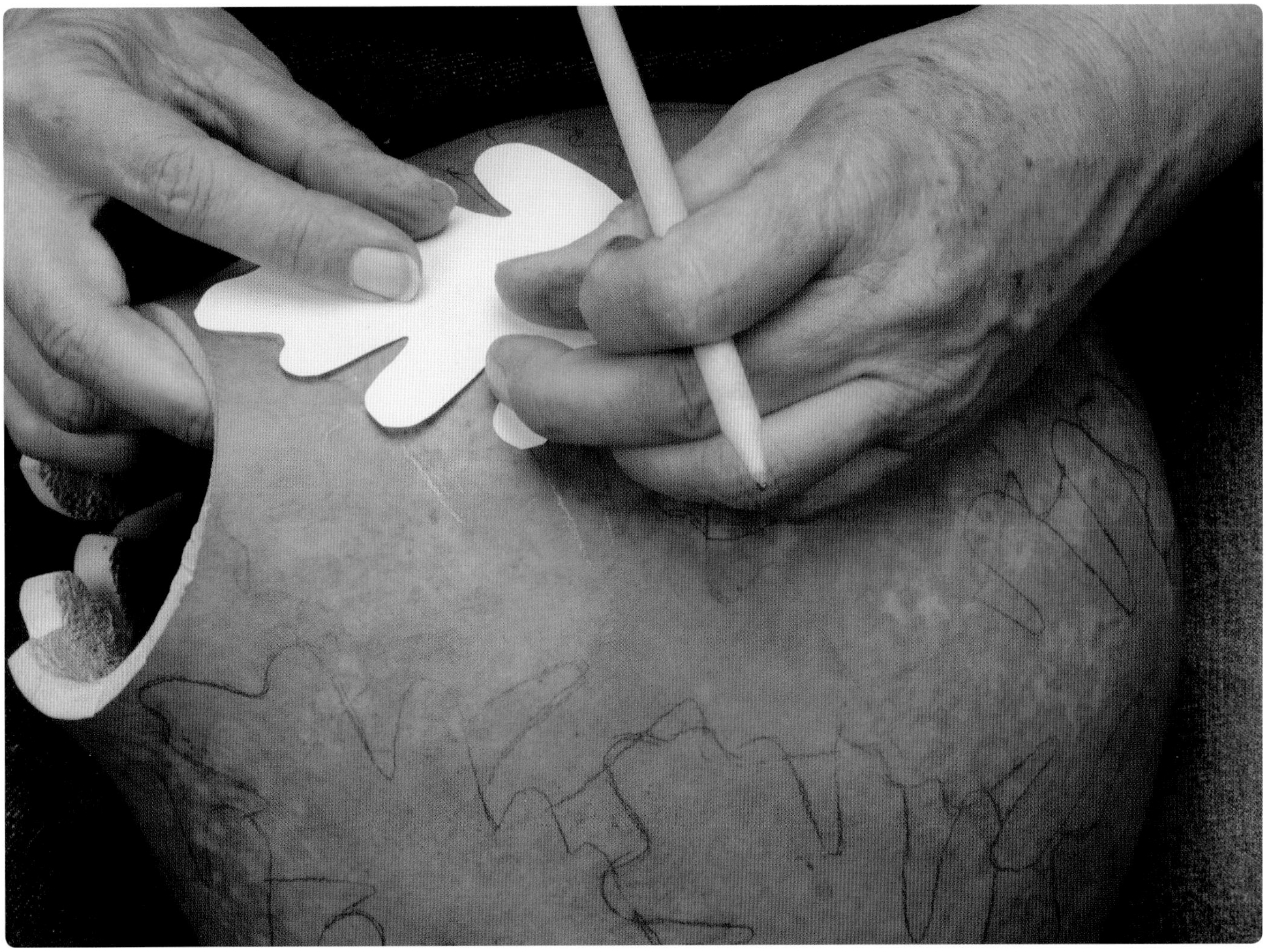

White oak leaf patterns.

Example of a good overlap in leaves.

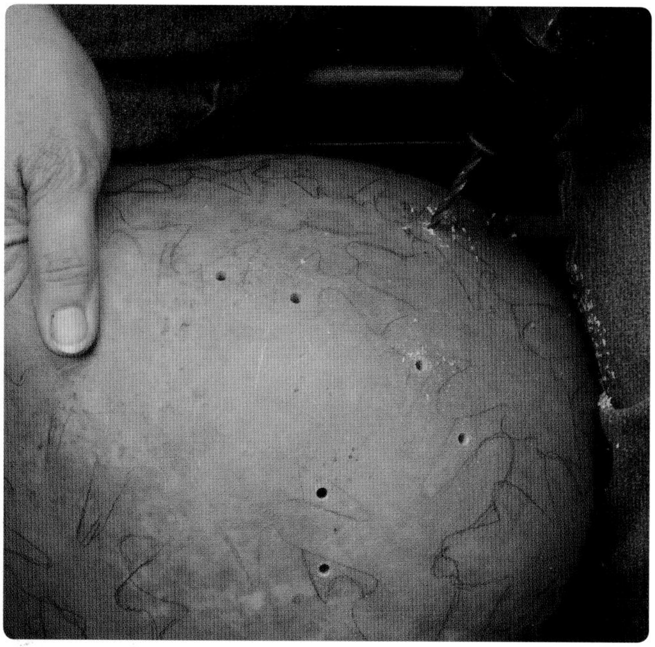

5. Drill holes in all open spaces between the leaves.

6. Insert your blade into each hole and cut out the space around the leaf. Cut continuously through the curve.

7. Carve veins using a rotary tool and a small round bur.

8. Remove gourd dust with a hair dryer or leaf blower.

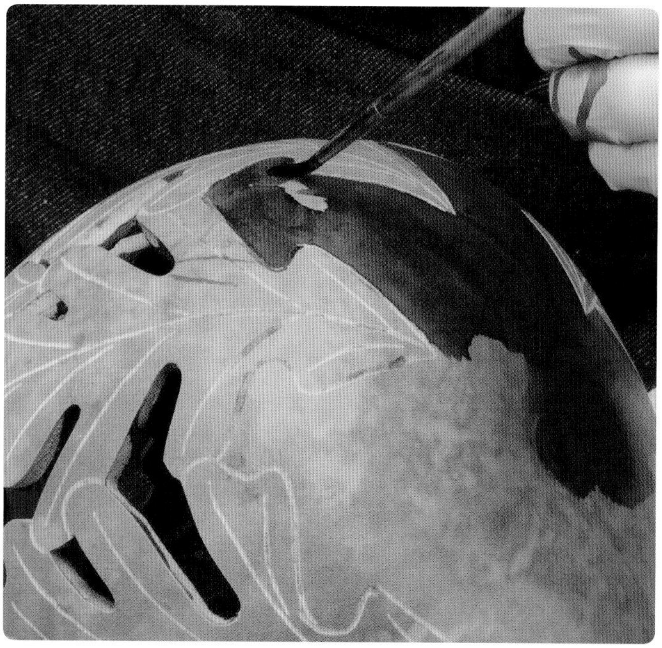

9. Dye the bottom of the gourd with a brown leather dye.

10. Color leaves one section at a time using yellow, green, orange, and red leather dyes.

a. First color a small section with yellow dye.

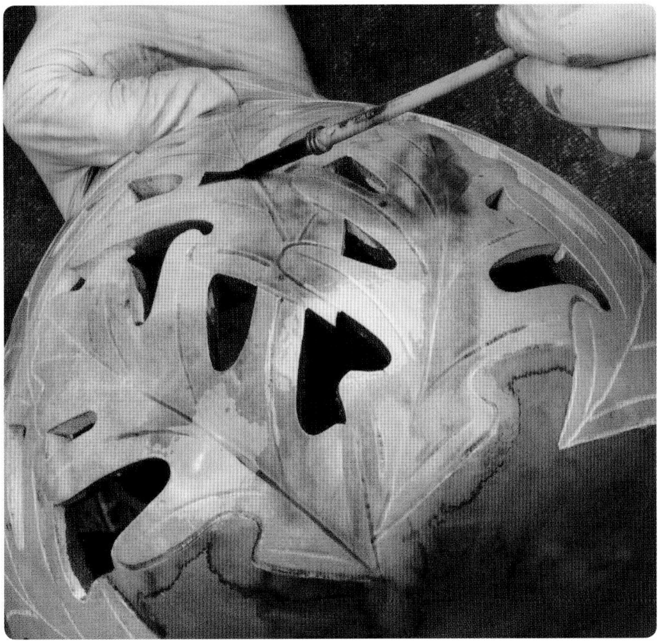

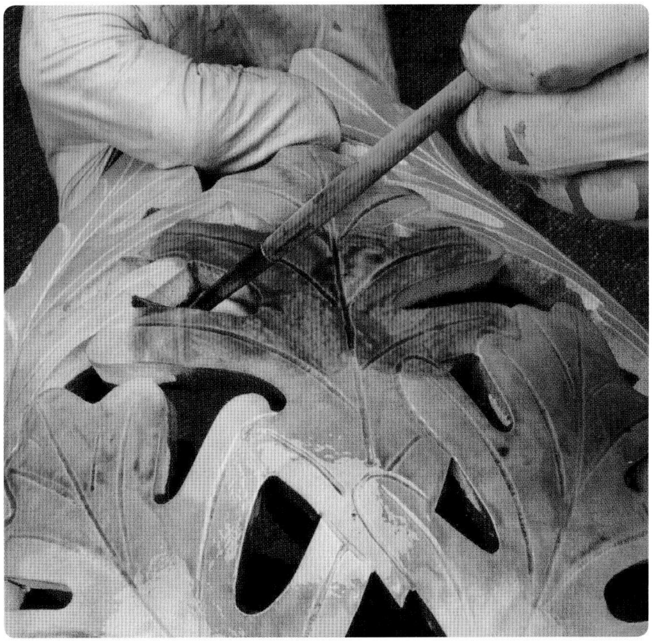

b. Dab or drop green and orange dye on leaves while the yellow dye is still wet. Note: Alcohol leather dyes dry very quickly, so work fast on small sections.

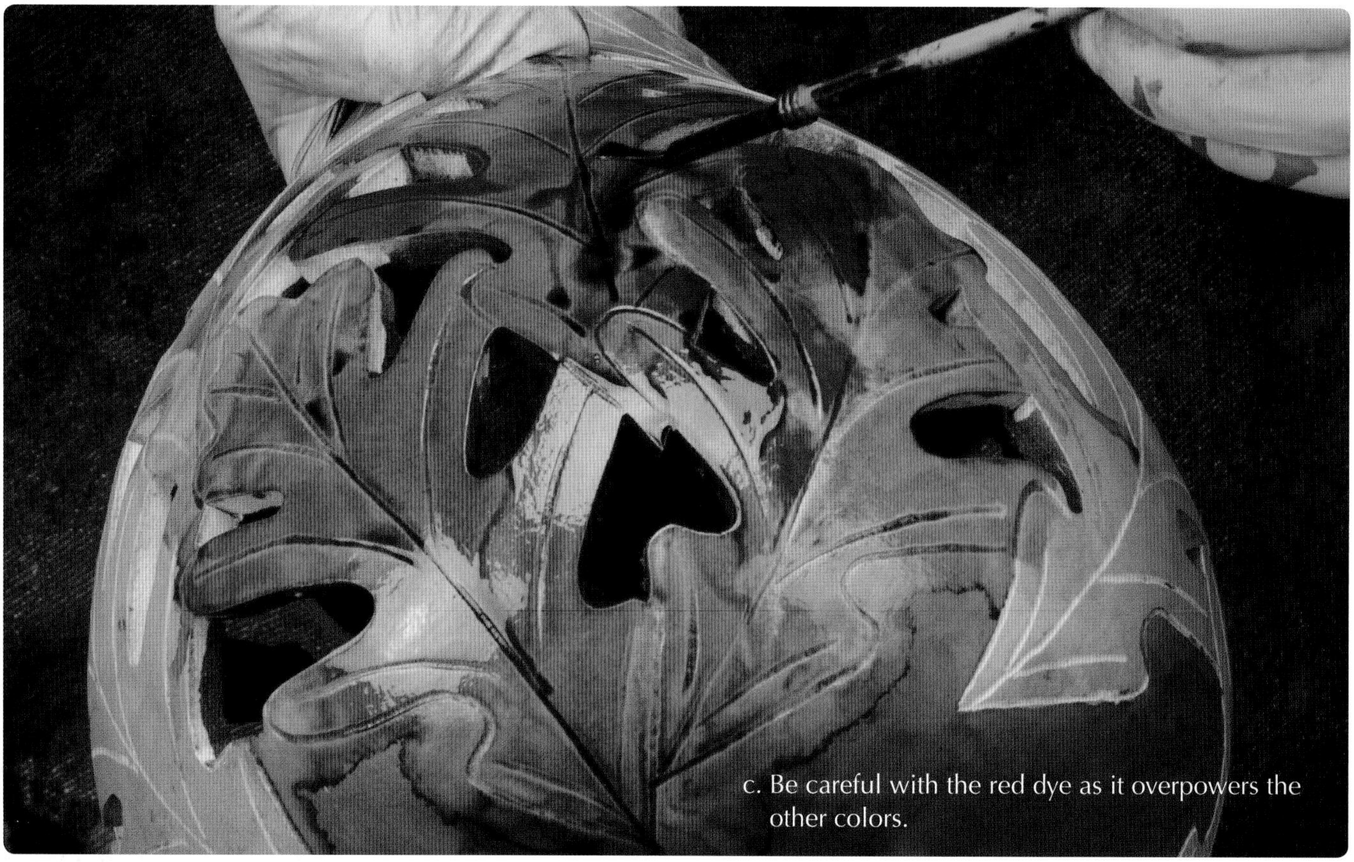

c. Be careful with the red dye as it overpowers the other colors.

d. If you have too much red dye, drop yellow dye to lighten the color.

e. Do not rub colors together, as this will create an unattractive "mud" color.

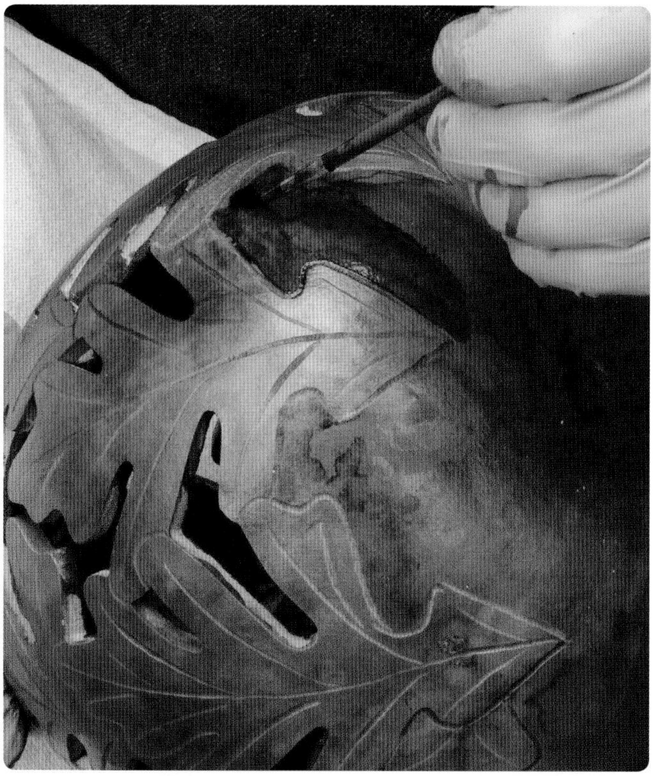

11. Re-dye the bottom of the gourd if necessary.

12. Color edges of leaves with medium brown leather dye.

13. Wipe a coat of Briwax over the gourd and then buff. The soft wax will fill in the areas you have cut out, so use a soft cloth to pull the wax out. Rub the extra wax on the outer side of the gourd leaves.

14. Use African bronze, Inca gold, and Verdigris Gilder's Paste to highlight leaves.

Lidded Leaf Bowl

This project creates the illusion of an intact gourd that has not been cut to remove the pulp and paint the inside. (This is, of course, an essential first step.) The lid on the bowl is cut in a way that it can be put back together like a puzzle. It is the placement of the leaves that allow you to create this effect.

Finished lidded leaf bowl.

Materials needed:

- Brown, Yellow, Green, Orange, and Red Leather dyes
- African Bronze, Inca Gold, and Verdigris Gilder's Paste
- Metallic Antique Copper Acrylic Paint
- Clear Drying Glue

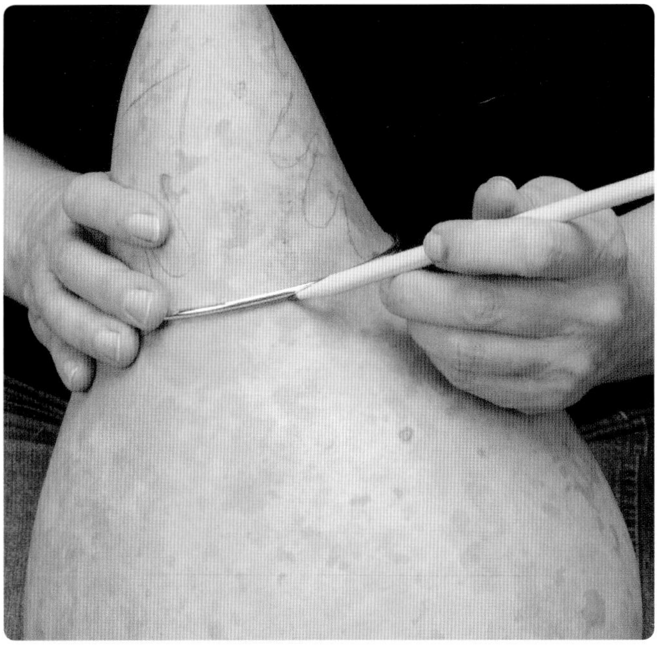

1. Draw a line around the gourd approximately where you want to separate the lid from the bowl. Sometimes I first draw one leaf and then use a metal ring to provide a guideline for my dividing line.

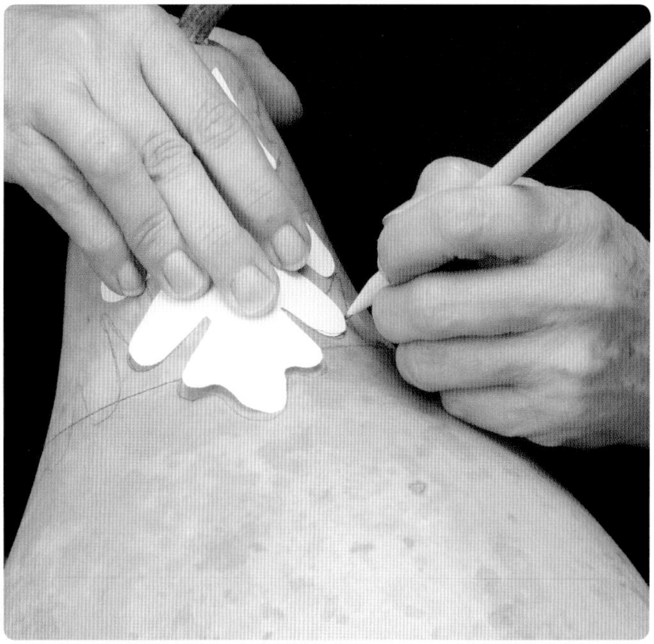

2. Draw your overlapping leaves facing down on the lid portion of the gourd. It's okay to go below your original guideline.

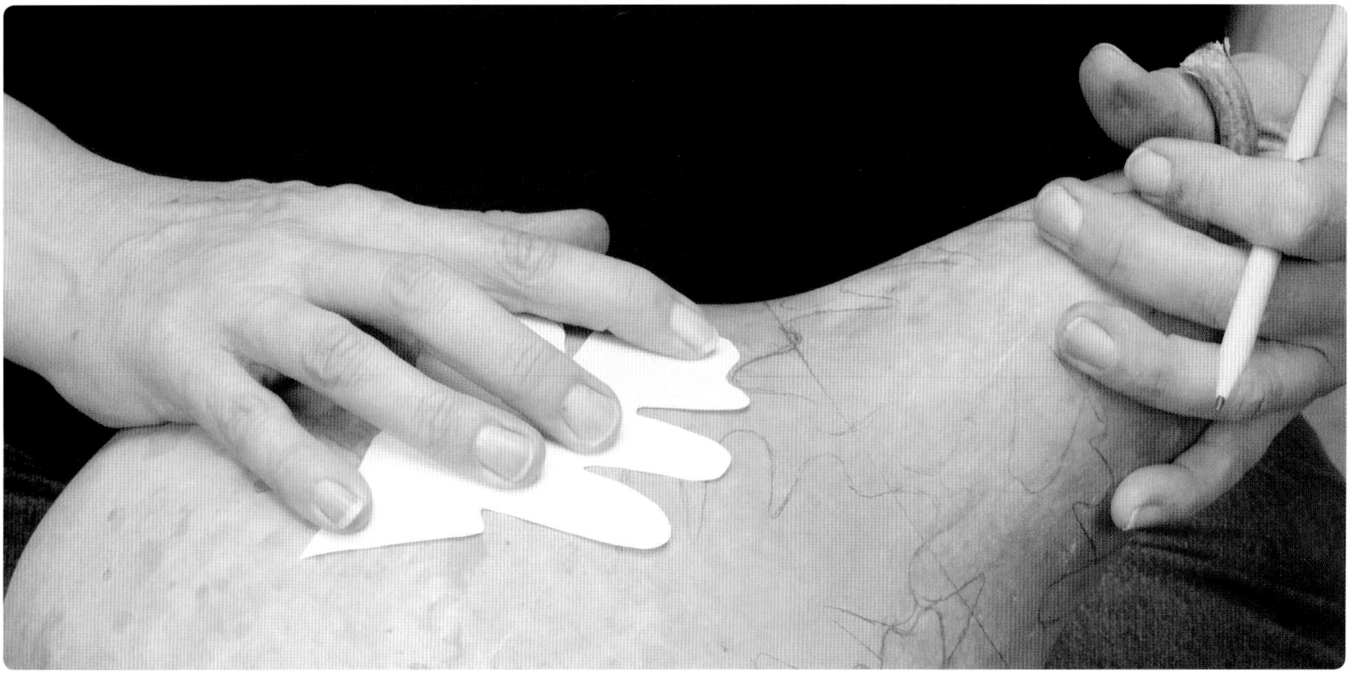

3. Draw your leaves facing up on the bowl. Do not overlap the lid and bowl leaves. Remember that the lid needs to come off.
4. You should be able to draw a line all the way around the gourd separating the top from the bottom (see dark line on following page).
5. Drill holes in the open space around your dark line.

Drawing leaves for a lidded leaf bowl.
Dark line separates lid from bowl.

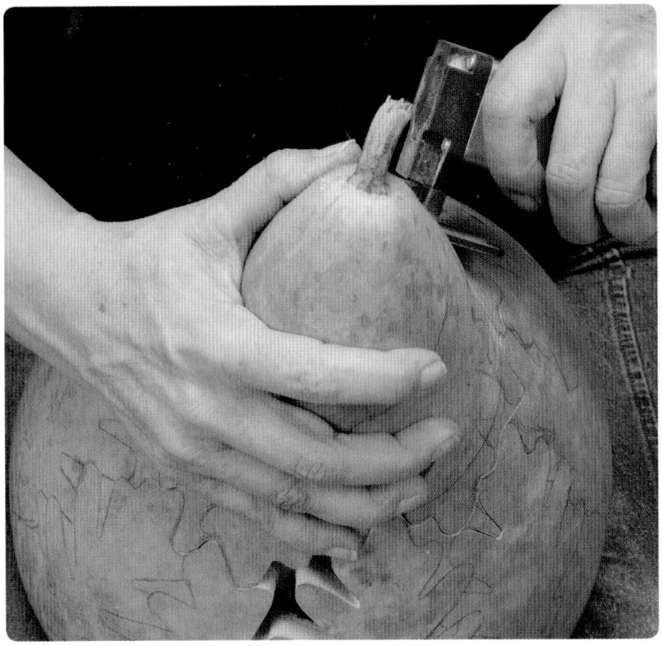

6. Cut around the dark line.

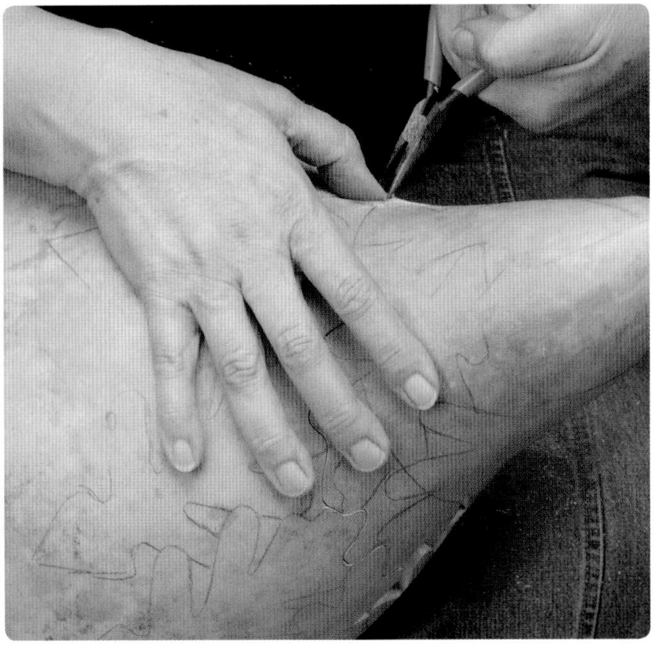

7. Sometimes the pieces will not fall out. Use a pair of pliers to pull out the cutout pieces.
8. If your gourd top does not come off, run an X-Acto knife to loosen any pulp.

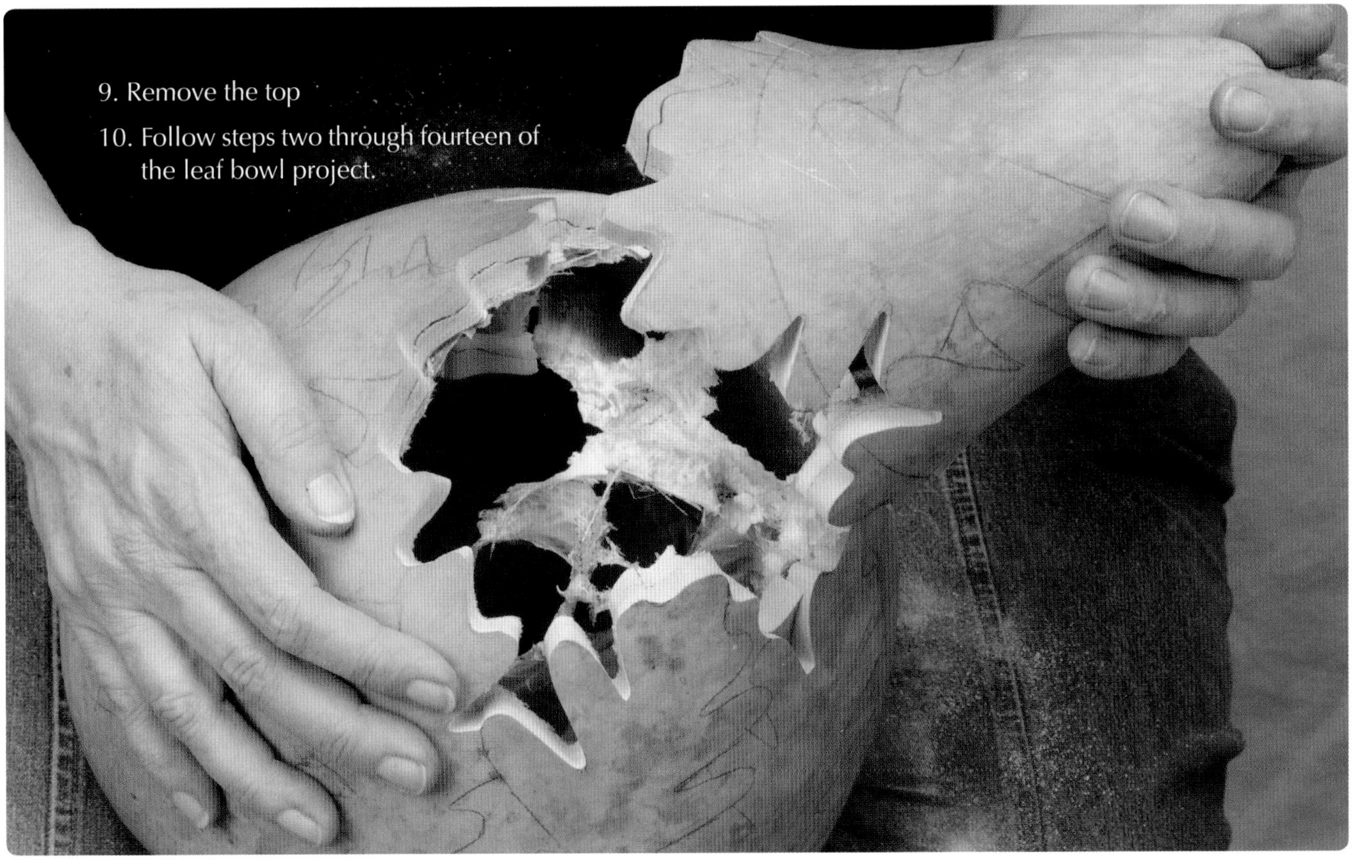

9. Remove the top
10. Follow steps two through fourteen of the leaf bowl project.

Oak leaf lampshade. *Courtesy of Susan M. Zanella*.

Autumn leaves lidded leaf bowl.

Penguin gourd leaf bowl on wooden platter.

CREATING SPOKES FOR WEAVING

Crafter A. B. Amis gave a demonstration at the Florida Gourd Society Festival on how to create basket spokes on the side of gourds. His approach took a lot of measuring. At home, I figured out how to create the spokes with less measuring.

Woven gourds with palm in florescence.

Materials needed:

- Flexible ruler
- 1″ tape
- 2″ tape
- Brown Leather dye
- Sealer

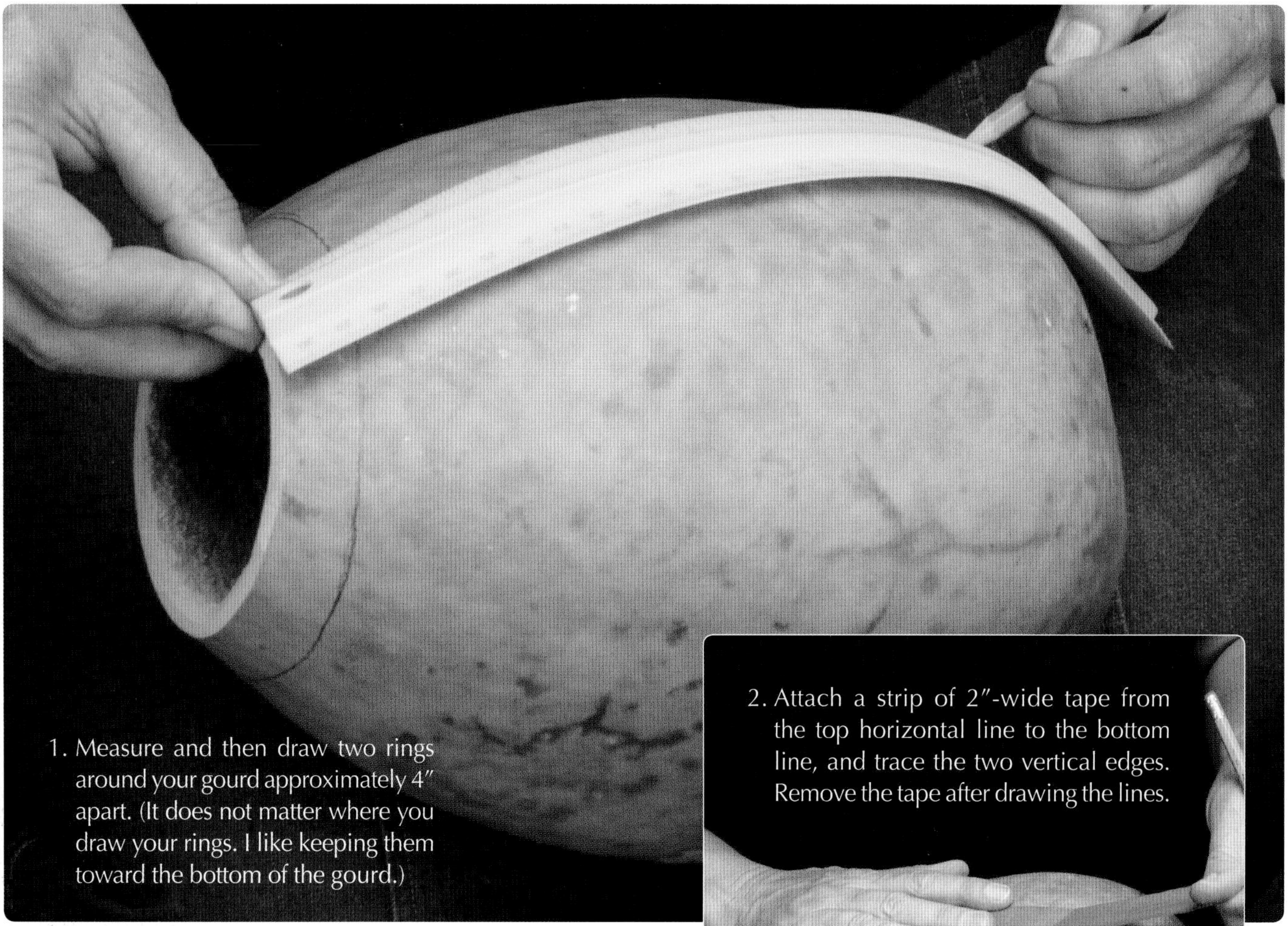

1. Measure and then draw two rings around your gourd approximately 4″ apart. (It does not matter where you draw your rings. I like keeping them toward the bottom of the gourd.)

2. Attach a strip of 2″-wide tape from the top horizontal line to the bottom line, and trace the two vertical edges. Remove the tape after drawing the lines.

3. Align the 1″ tape to the outside of the lines drawn in Step 2, and draw the outside lines.
4. Repeat steps 2 and 3 around the gourd, removing and reusing the tape as you go. (The advantage of using tape is that you can readjust to compensate for the gourd's irregular shape.)

Note: The last 1″ strip of tape may not fit, so adjust the size of the 2″ strips on either side.

5. Draw an "X" inside all the 1" strips.

6. Drill a hole in each 1" strip.

7. Cut out the 1"-wide strips to create your spokes. The mini-jigsaw will make 90-degree turns.

8. Dye the gourd with medium brown leather dye.

9. Seal the gourd.

10. Your gourd is ready to weave.

Fish Tales

Earlier in the book, I mentioned that I bought my first saw after seeing Jeanne Ames' "Fish Tale" article in the 2003 March/April issue of *Expression* magazine. Jeanne has given me permission to include her Fish Tales as a project. I hope you enjoy making them as much as I do.

The finished Fish Tale Gourd.

Materials needed:

- Black Acrylic Paint and Clear Drying Glue
- Yellow, Pool, Bottle, Stream, and Sail Boat Blue Adirondack Inks
- Spray Sealer

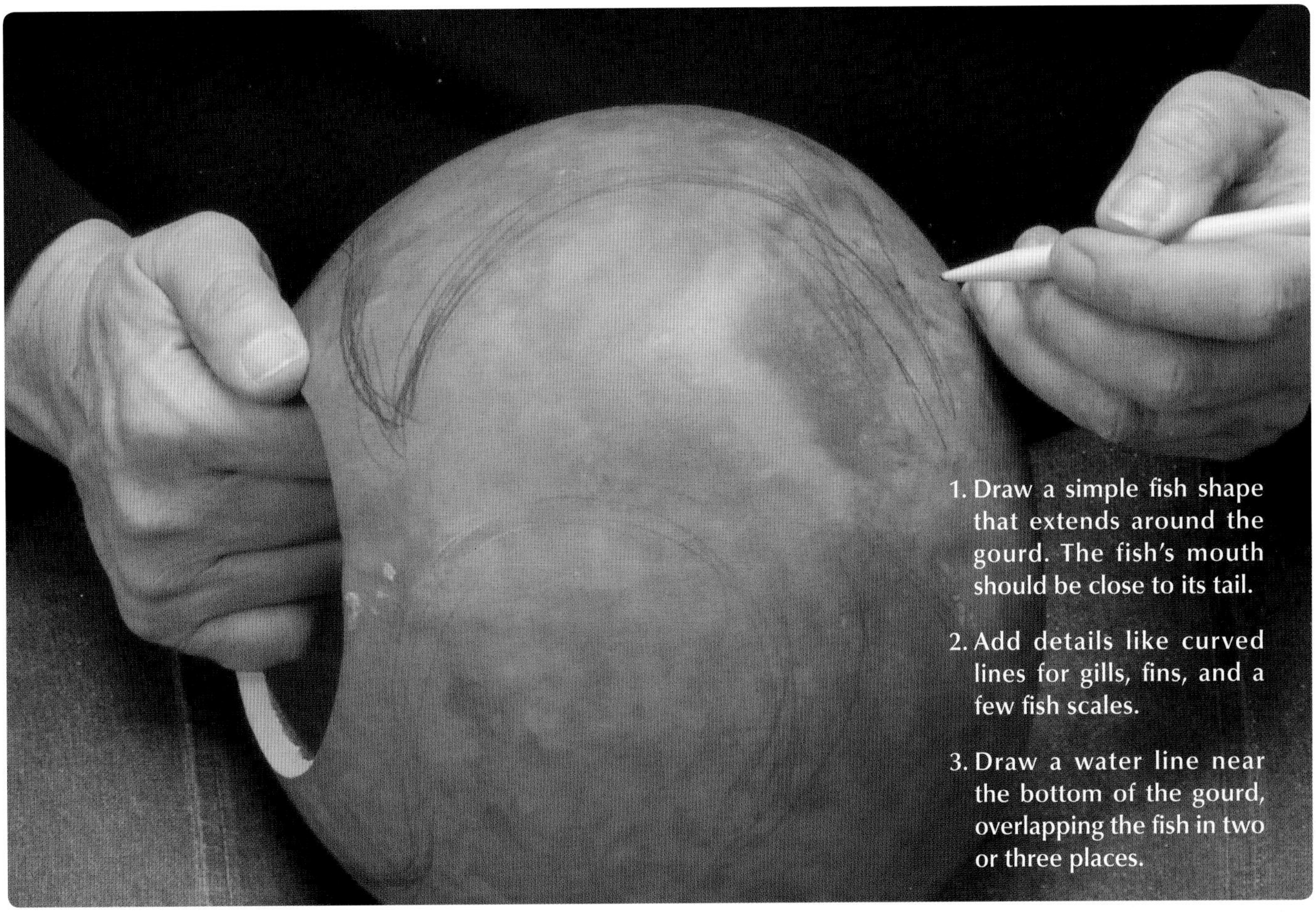

1. Draw a simple fish shape that extends around the gourd. The fish's mouth should be close to its tail.
2. Add details like curved lines for gills, fins, and a few fish scales.
3. Draw a water line near the bottom of the gourd, overlapping the fish in two or three places.

4. Drill a 1/2″ hole for the fish eye.
5. Drill holes in all the spaces that are not fish or water.
6. Cut out the fish gills and lines in the fins and tail.
7. Cut out all the spaces that are not fish or water.

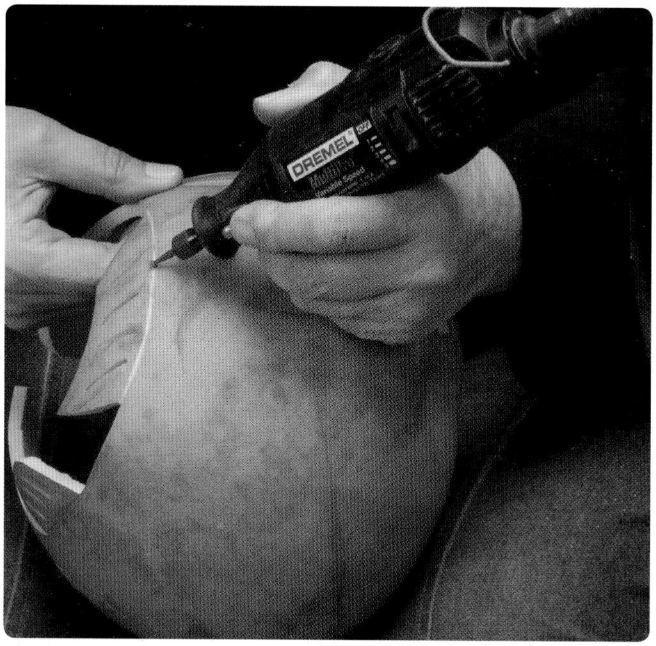

8. Carve lines to distinguish the fish from the water.

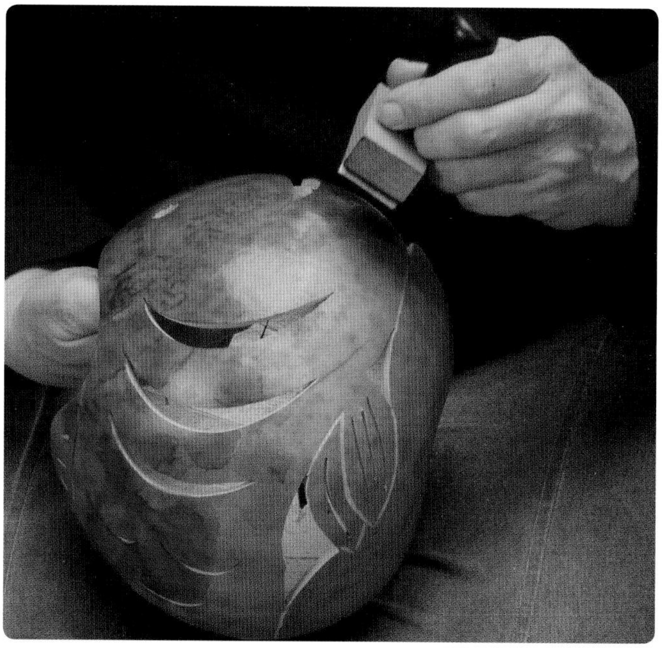

9. Alternating between yellow, bottle, and stream, stamp the Adirondack inks on the fish.

10. Stamp the water with Sail Boat Blue Adirondack Ink.

11. Seal with a spray. If you use a rub-on sealer, you will rub off the mottle pattern you created by stamping the ink.

Luminaries

In February 2011, in the middle of the Wuertzs Gourd Festival, I spoke to fellow gourder Jim Widdes about my book project. With customers milling around, he was kind enough to give me some of his time. He thought there should be an entire book on gourd luminaries since they were getting so popular. He recommended that I buy an expensive book — that turned out to be written in Korean. While I can't read a single word, I love to see the expressions on the faces of my family and friends when they open it. Thank you, Jim, not only for taking time to talk to me, but for providing me with a "coffee-table" book that always starts conversations. This luminary project is for you.

A gourd luminary is a gourd with designs that are illuminated by a light source, e.g., electric light, candlelight.

An easy way to create a luminary is to drill holes either in a specific pattern or randomly and then add a light. More advanced designs move beyond creating holes to creating patterns. When cutting out larger designs, you need to think about how they will affect the lighting patterns.

I have discovered different ways to light up your gourds.

· The simple battery tea light: These can be purchased in many stores, but they do not emit a lot of light (I have been using them inside Jack-O-Lanterns.)

· Create a nightlight: If you don't want to locate all the pieces, you can purchase a kit from Arizona Gourds.

· A combination of a plug with a single light bulb socket: I found a plug and socket with a stand at Eli Smucker's gourd farm. It is a molded stand and six feet of wire cordage with a plug, switch and bulb socket. The stand easily holds a gourd from 3" to 10" in circumference. It takes a 2.5" diameter hole in the bottom of the gourd.

· A swag kit from your local hardware store.

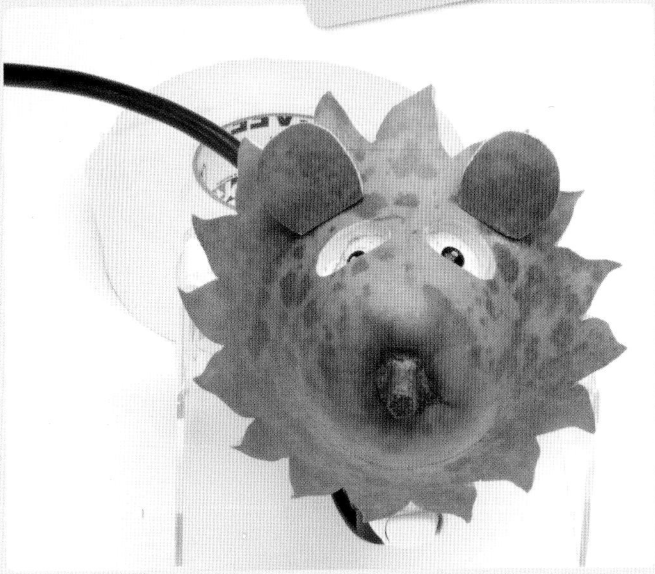

Lion Nightlight. *Courtesy of JoAnne Phelps.*

Mouse Nightlight. *Courtesy of JoAnne Phelps.*

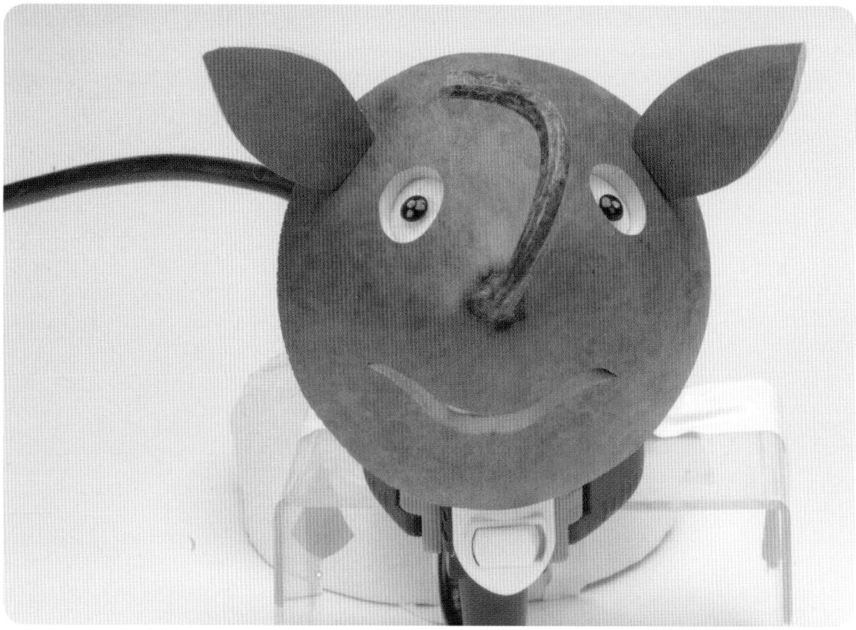

There are different ways to light up your gourds. For this project, I rebuilt a pendant light or lamp fixture that I found on a sale table of a thrift shop.

1,000 Holes

Although this first project does not need a mini-jigsaw, I had to include it for its simplicity and beauty.

Cannonball gourd nightlight. I used a 25-watt chandelier bulb for this picture.

Materials needed:

- Cannonball gourd
- Drill Bits in Assorted Sizes (1/16″ to 1/2″)
- 2-1/2″ Hole Saw with Pilot Bit (optional)
- Stand and Electrical Plug
- Dark Red Leather Dye
- Cranberry Design Master Spray
- Sealer

What You Do:

1. Drill a 2-1/2″-hole in the bottom of a cannonball gourd. If you do not want to invest in a 2-1/2″-hole saw, then draw the circle and cut it out with your mini-jigsaw.
2. Remove pulp.

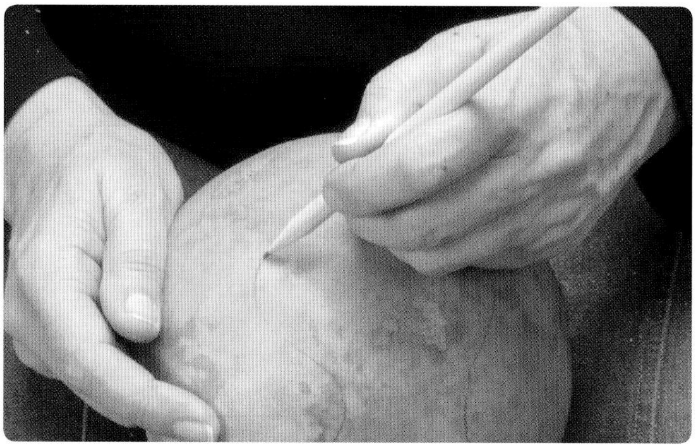

3. Draw five wavy circles, which will create sections.

4. Starting with the largest bit, drill random holes in the top section.
5. Skip a section and drill holes in the third ring.
6. Skip a section and drill holes in the fifth ring.
7. Change drill bits, and drill holes again in the 1st, 3rd, and 5th sections.

8. Enhance sections by carving the five wavy circles.

9. Use a copper scrubbie or a toilet brush to smooth the inside of the gourd; remove all of the pulp residue.

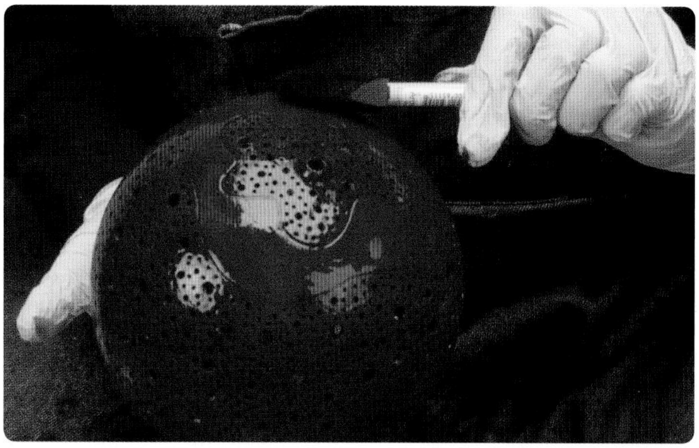

10. Dye with Dark Red leather dye

11. To enhance the red, spray with Cranberry Design Master spray

12. Seal with Deft.

13. Mount on stand.

I noticed on the Gourd Art Enthusiast's website that gourd artists were experimenting with glass beads in the holes. I experimented with beads, and worked out the ratio of bead size to drilled hole. I have included it to save others some time. I also found it was easy to insert the bead in the hole by placing the bead on the end of an awl.

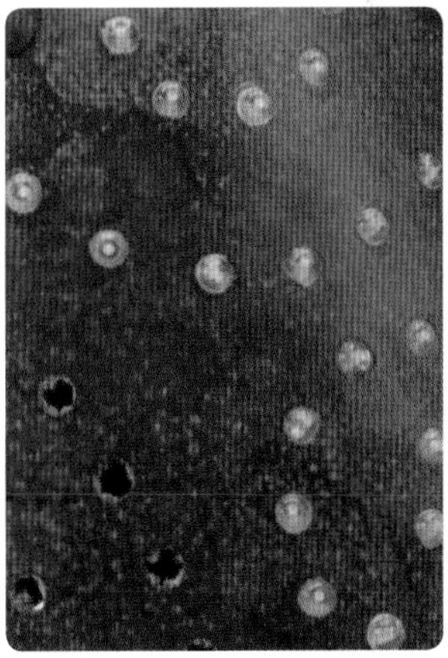

Lighted Spirals

After drilling my 1,000 hole-luminary, I started experimenting by cutting out simple shapes, e.g., stars, teardrops of varying sizes, and spirals. My favorite look was the spiral patterns, but I broke a few gourds in the cutting process. I found that I could consistently cut the spiral if I divided it into three sections. First, I cut the inside curve, then turned the gourd and cut the middle section, and finally the outside section. If I wanted the spiral to be wide, I would cut the inside line and then the outside edge. That way there is less pressure on the cut portion of the spiral.

Spiral cut-out nightlight.

Materials needed:

- Cannonball Gourd
- 2-1/2″ Hole Saw with Pilot Bit (optional)
- Stand and Electrical Plug
- Blue Leather Dye
- Deep Blue Design Master Spray
- Sealer

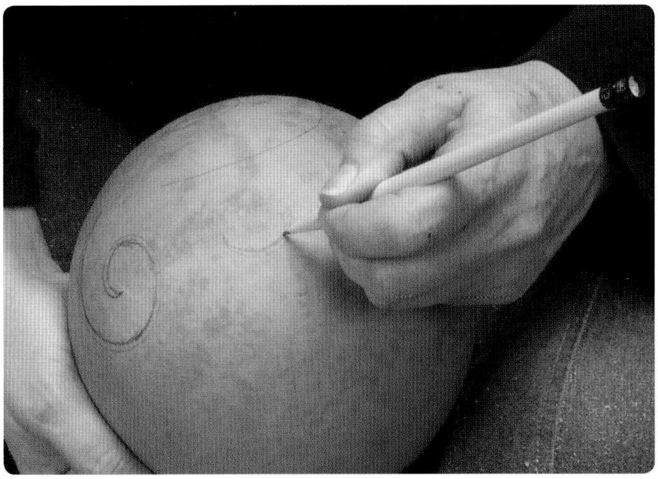

1. Drill a 2-1/2″ hole in the bottom of a cannon ball gourd. If you do not want to invest in a 2-1/2″ hole saw, draw the circle and cut it out with your mini-jigsaw.
2. Remove pulp.
3. Draw different size spirals.
4. Drill a hole in each spiral. You can use a 1/16″ bit.

5. Cut out spirals. I noticed that the spirals would "pop" after they were cut and "free."

6. Dye with Blue leather dye. This is a difficult color to use on a gourd. I enhance the color with Design Master Deep Blue spray

7. Mount on light stand.

Displaying spirals on the wall.

Pendant Light

At my local hardware store, there was a sale on pendant lights. I bought three to create special lighting over my computer work area. After removing the boxing material, I found that the glass globe was the same size as my cannonball gourds.

I had just finished the 1,000-holes and spirals projects, so, for this design, I decided to combine them.

Cannonball gourd pendant light.

Materials needed:

- Cannonball Gourd
- 1/18″ hole saw drill bit
- Drill bits in assorted sizes (1/16″, 5/64″, 3/32″, 7/64″)
- Honey Leather Dye
- Sealer
- Rapidograph pens

1. Measure holes in the glass globe. The top hole was 1-1/8″ and the bottom opening was 4″ on this particular pendant light.

2. Draw a 4″ circle on the bottom of the gourd and cut out.

3. Remove pulp.

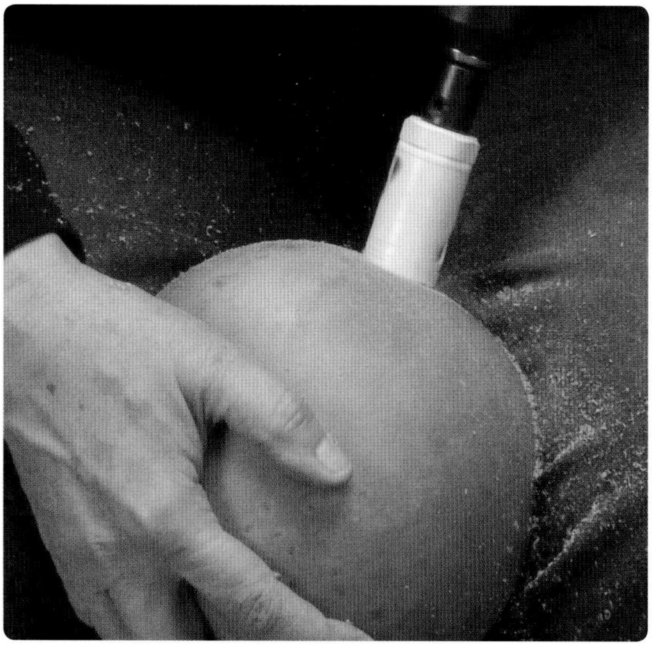

4. Drill a 1-1/8″ hole in top of the gourd.

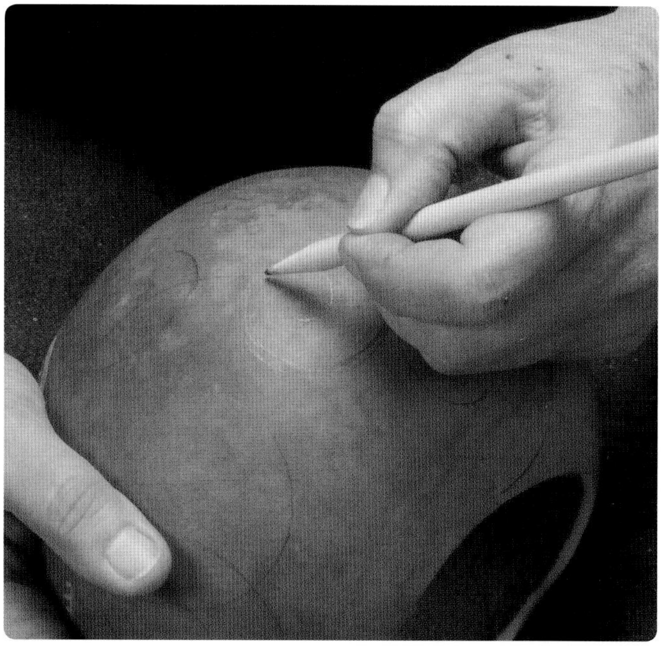

5. Draw overlapping spirals in different sizes.

6. Gently carve some spirals.

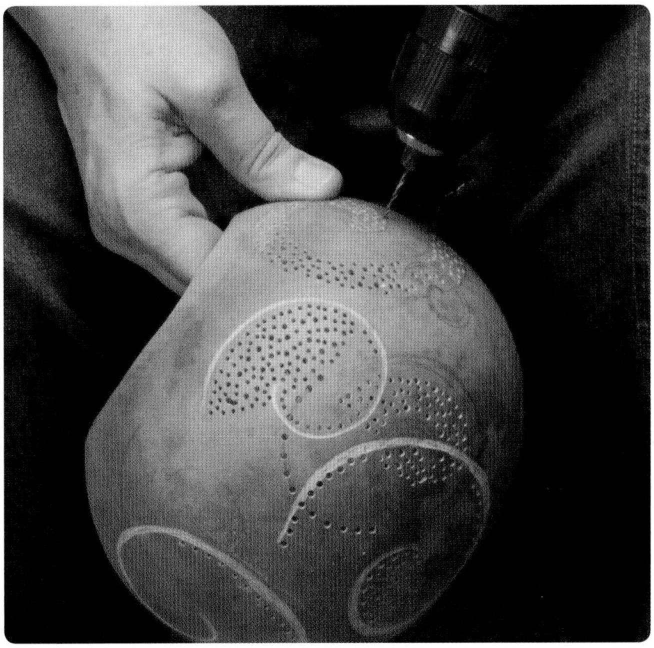

7. Drill holes following the spiral patterns using different drill bits for different spirals.
8. Fill in some areas with assorted size holes.

9. Smooth the inside of the gourd to remove hole-pulp residue.
10. Cut out remaining spirals.

11. Use Honey leather dye to enhance the natural color of the gourd.
12. Seal with lacquer.

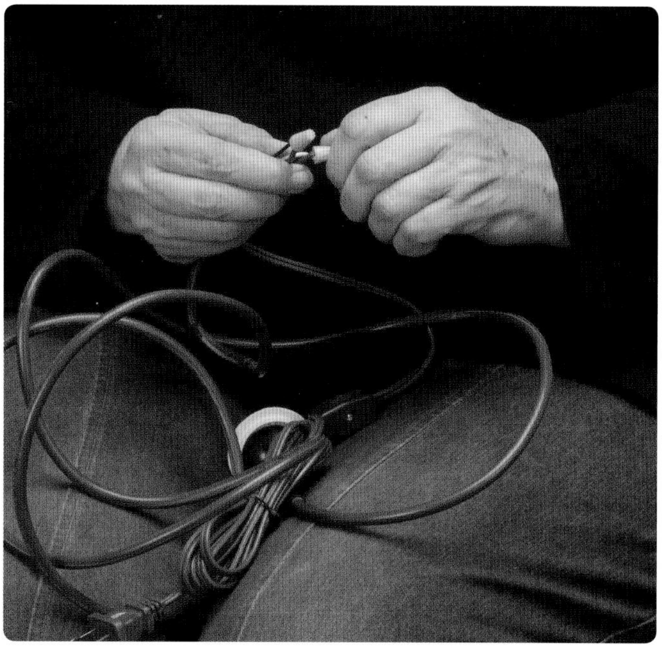

13. Splice the pendant light cord with a six-foot cord with plug and switch.

14. To hide the spliced area, slide a small banana gourd onto the cord before splicing. The gourd should be dyed and have a 1/4″ hole drilled through. Use Quikwood® to keep the small gourd in place.

15. Highlight the carved spirals with a rapidographic pen and black ink.

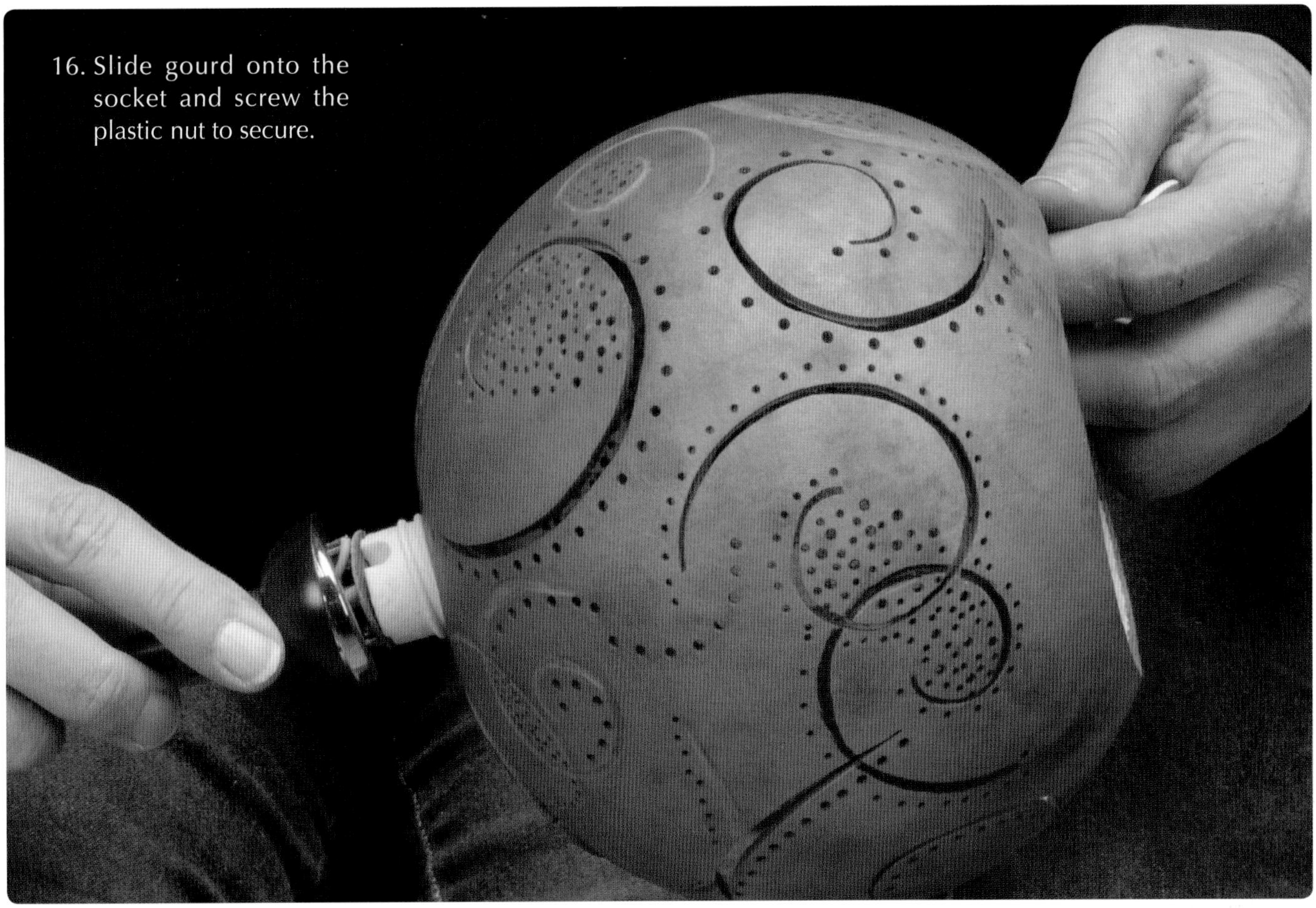

16. Slide gourd onto the socket and screw the plastic nut to secure.

You can suspend the light from a cup hook, curved rod, or even outside on a tree branch. I can't wait to show my pendant light off at the next Cherokee Gourd Gathering.

My Pendant Light patterns.

JACK-O-LANTERNS

I love making jack-o-lantern gourds! They are one of the first things I created to give to family and friends. I designed a Jack face on my square for the Gourdpatch Quilt that was created by 112 artists because it captures my love of jacks. I sell "Mr. Jack" at local and regional craft shows. They are fun to make and people love their faces. Buyers come every year to take home another "Mr. Jack" for their collections. This year, I realized I had created eleven unique faces, so I combined them to create Mr. Jack and Sons, a collection of all my faces on one gourd.

When making Mr. Jacks, the biggest challenge is cleaning out the gourd. This step is the time-consuming part of any gourd project. I have tried to come up with better methods than handscraping or even using a drill with the gourd cleaning balls. My favorite is the "water method."

Personalities of Mr. Jack.

Materials needed:

- Any gourd
- Orange Leather Dye
- Minwax® Wipe-On Polyurethane

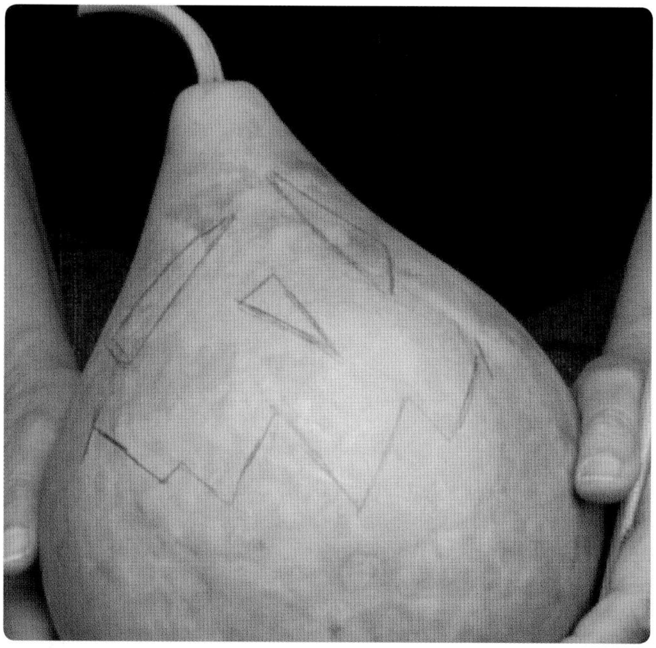

1. Draw a jack-o-lantern face on the gourd.
2. Drill holes in the cutout areas.

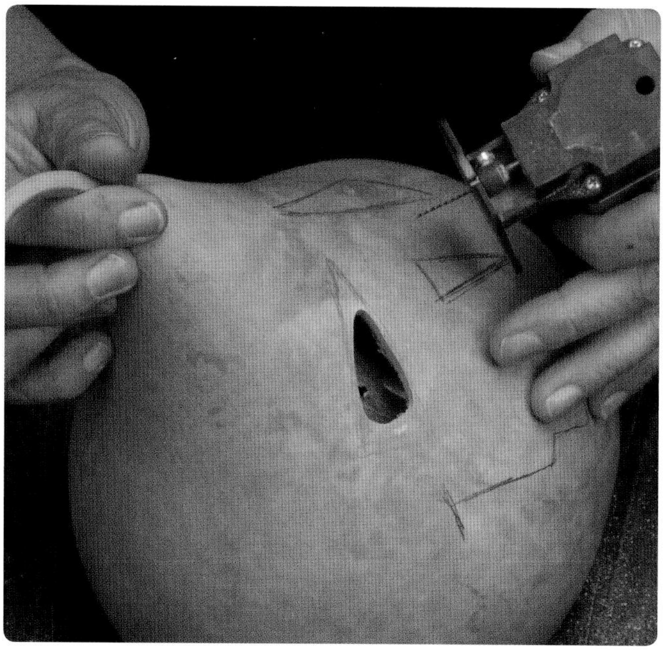

3. Cut out face parts smoothing all angles.

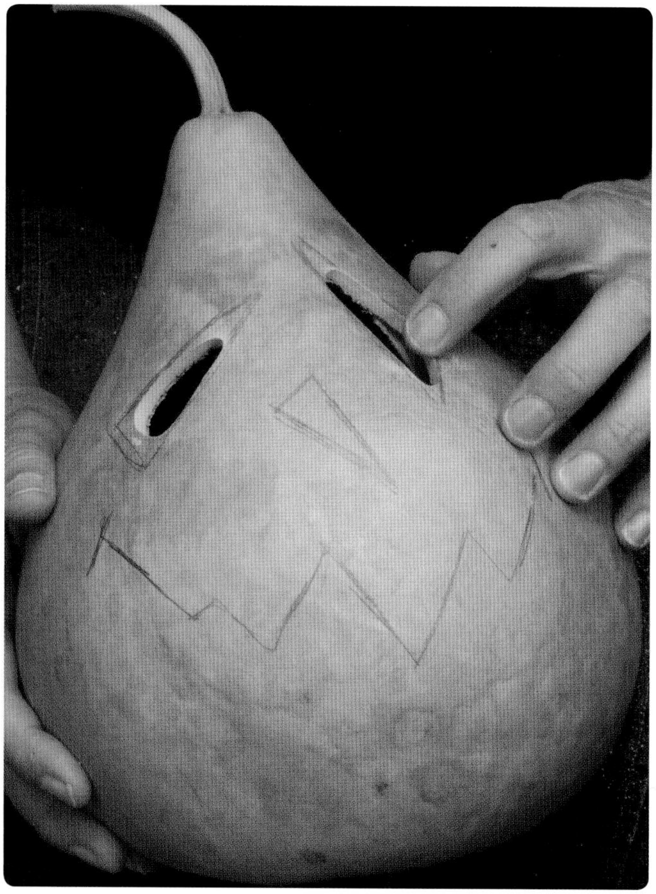

4. Clean the inside of the gourd using the water method.
   a. Fill the gourd with water.
   b. Wait three days.
   c. Easily scrap out pulp with the flat section of a canning jar lid.
   d. If you do not plan to paint the inside of your Mr. Jack, refill it with a half-and-half solution of bleach and water. This makes the interior of the gourd a consistent whitish color. If you use bleach, you will need to do a final soaking in vinegar to stop the action of the bleach or it will eat through the gourd.
5. Finish cutting out the faces – the sharp angles.
6. Dye with Orange leather dye.
7. Seal with wipe-on polyurethane.

Mr. Jack Gourd Identification Chart

Many gourd books have gourd identification charts, so I created my own "Mr. Jack Gourd Identification Chart." I hope you enjoy them.

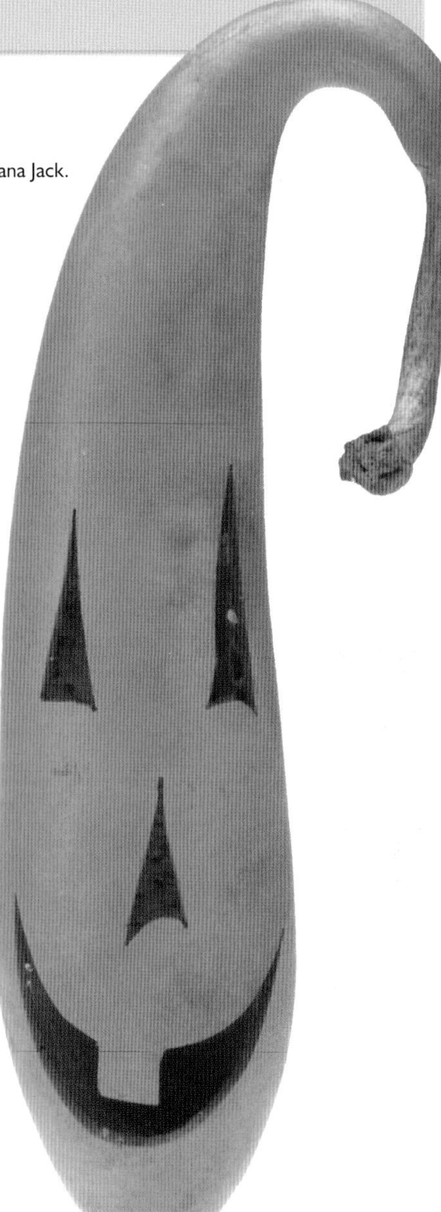

Banana Jack.

Apple Jack.

Cannonball Jacks.

African Wartie Jack.

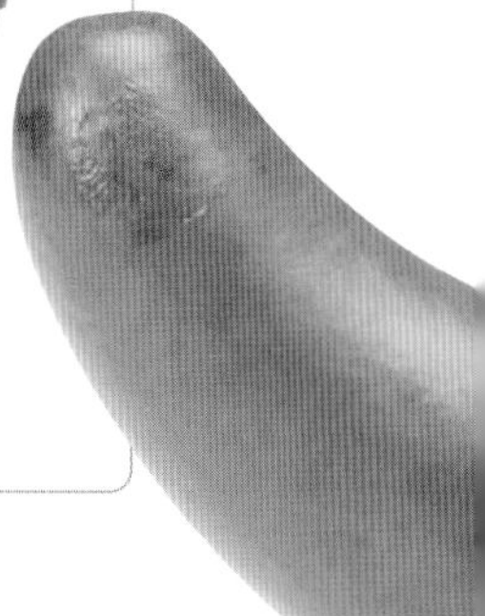

American Wartie Jack.

Beehive Jack.

Milk Bottle Jack.

Penguin Jack.

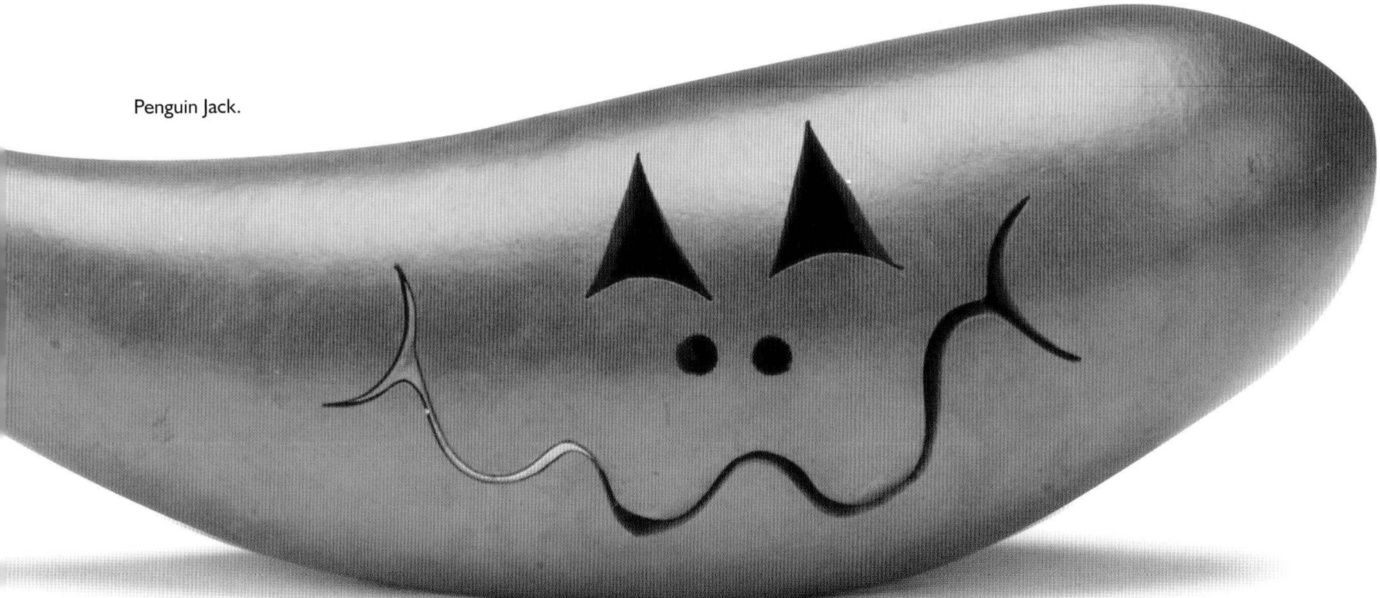

Tobacco Box Jack.

Canteen Jack.

Comparing Canteen and Tobacco Box gourds.

Chinese Bottle Jack.

Dipper Jack.

Martian Jack.

Copper Canyon Kettle Jack.

Snake Jack.

Goose or Swan Jack.

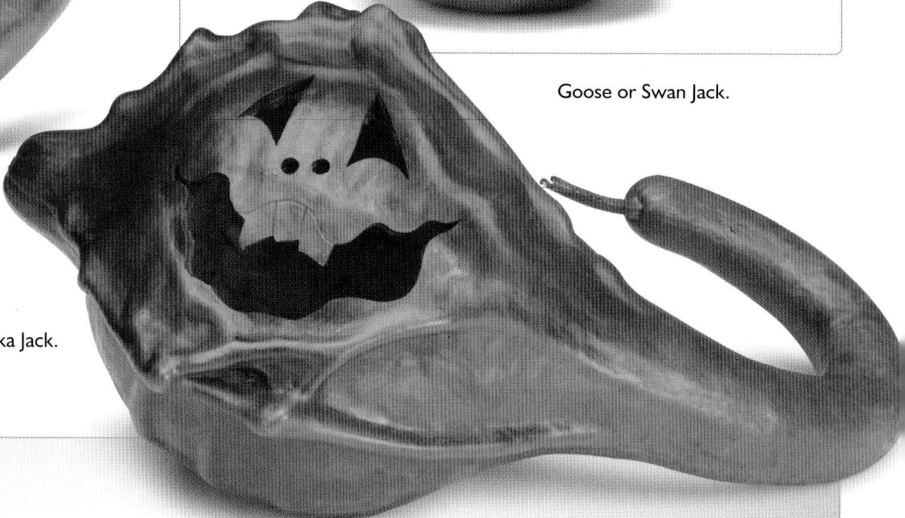

Maranka Jack.

Wanna-Be Jacks. From left to right: Giant Bushel, Indonesian Bottle, African Wine Kettle, Bushel, Zucca, and Hybrid.

The Appendix

Gallery

When I look at the types of gourd art I create, I realize I want people to first recognize it as a gourd that has been enhanced. So my goal is to take a natural gourd and turn it into a functional vessel, a whimsical object, or a three-dimensional art piece while maintaining the gourd's identity. The gallery showcases gourds that have been cut, but also wood-burned, carved, woven, and embellished.

I hope you enjoy them.

Red Oak Leaf Bowl. *Courtesy of Susan M. Zanella.*

Winter Moon.

Mini-jigsaw Filigree.

White Oak Leaf Bowl.
Courtesy of Susan M. Zanella.

Large Bushel Gourd – Lidded Leaf Bowl.

Autumn Leaves.

Nesting Jacks.

Six Nesting Jacks.

Out for a Ride. Circle cut-out. *Courtesy of Susan M. Zanella.*

Chattering Squirrels. *Courtesy of Jayne Wright.*

Poinsettias.
Courtesy of JoAnne Phelps.

Fish Tales I. *Courtesy of Jeanne Ames.*

Fish Tales II. *Courtesy of Jeanne Ames.*

Frog Reunion. *Courtesy of Jeanne Ames.*

Pacific Northwest Frogs. *Courtesy of Jeanne Ames.*

Gourd Vine Puzzle. *Courtesy of Lorraine Haggard.*

Gourd Puzzle with insets.

Flower Project.

Flower Project. *Courtesy of Susan M. Zanella.*

Flower Project. *Courtesy of Lorraine Haggard.*

Hanging Pendant Light.

Table Lights or Night Lights.
Courtesy of Lorraine Haggard.

Table Lights or Night Lights.
Courtesy of Lorraine Haggard.

Courtesy of Lorraine Haggard.

Table Lights or Night Lights. *Courtesy of Lorraine Haggard.*

Thunder Drums.
Courtesy of Susan M. Zanella.

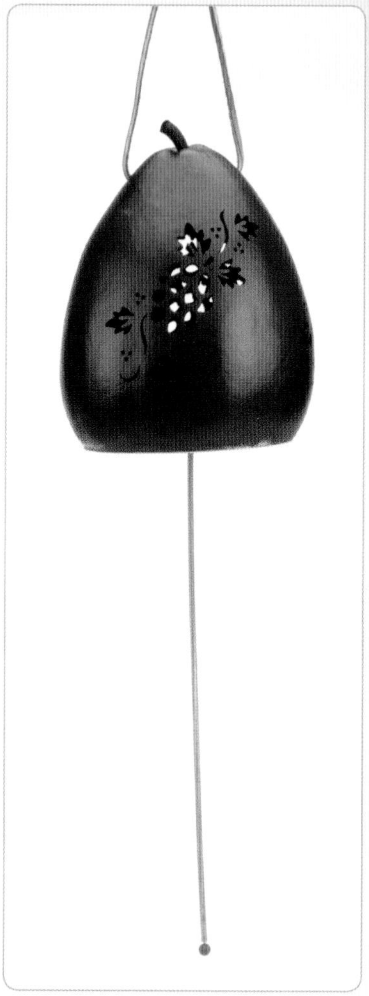
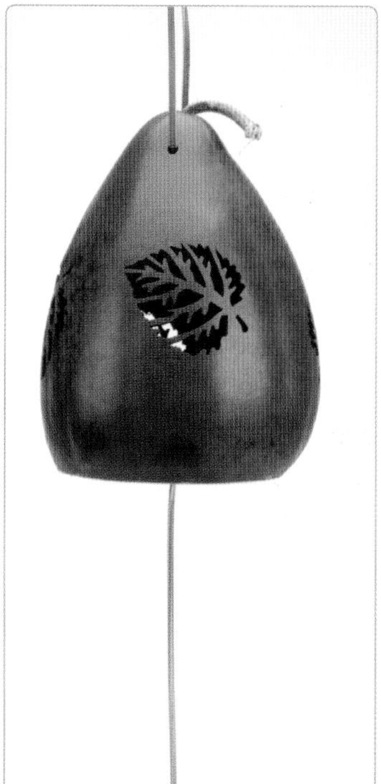
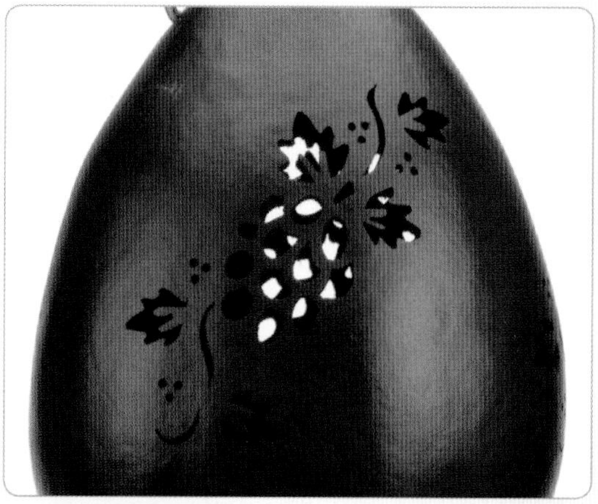
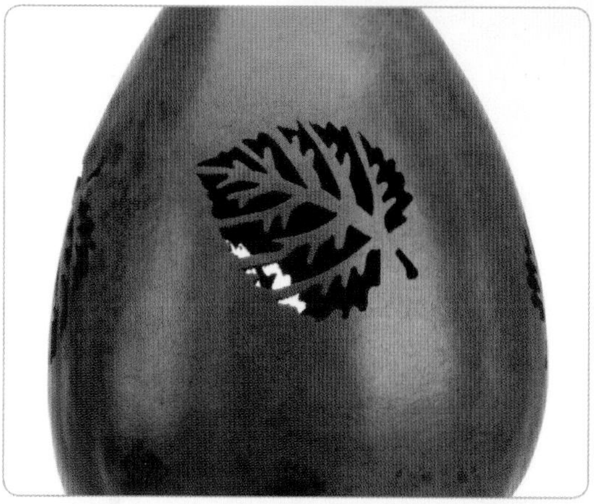

Biographies of Contributing Artists

Jeanne Ames

Dr. Jeanne Ames is a gourd artist and Chiropractor from San Diego, California. She is a member of the Misti Washington Gourd and Basket Guild in Encinitas, California.

Her interest in art began twenty years ago when she started collecting masks from around the world.

Jeanne was introduced to gourds in March 2000 through her good friends, Paul and Kathi Klopfenstein, and began creating her own gourd masks and vessels. She discovered the versatility of gourds and began experimenting with different techniques.

Some are carved, cut, or woodburned. Some are adorned with jewelry, beads, feathers, or natural fibers. Acrylic paint and leather dyes are used to achieve the vibrant color. All are unique and the shape of the gourd determines the character of the piece.

She was a featured artist on *The Carol Duvall Show* on HGTV and has exhibited her work at juried exhibits, such as the Talmadge Art Show in San Diego, Artwear San Diego at the Holiday Inn Express in Point Loma, and Le Cirque de l'Art in La Jolla. Her fish tale gourds were featured in and on the cover of *Expression* magazine. "Pacific Northwest Frogs" was featured in *The Complete Book of Gourd Carving* by Jim Widess and Ginger Summit.

Lorraine Haggard

Lorraine is a classically trained visionary artist and teacher who has added gourds to her repertoire of artistic expression. Born in Pittsburgh, Pennsylvania, as a child she studied art at the Carnegie Museum in Pittsburgh and then went on to get her Fine Art Degree at Seton Hill College in Art Education. Over the years she has studied commercial art at The Art Institute of Pittsburgh and classical realistic oil painting at The Brandywine Atelier. Lorraine has also taken many art workshops for enrichment.

Lorraine was first introduced to gourd art three years ago, and there was an instant connection to the natural, organically shaped gourd canvas. With her background in art forms, techniques, and materials, Lorraine began creating on this new three-dimensional canvas. At the present time, she is a part-time art teacher at a private school and a full-time gourd artist.

Ken Heeter

Ken and his wife Agnes have been married fifty years and live in Bel Air, Maryland. They feel blessed to have their three children and nine grandchildren living nearby. A Radiologic Technologist for fifty-two years, Ken continues to fill in when needed at a local hospital where he has been employed for thirty-two years. He has been painting with watercolor and oil paints for over sixty years and continues to take watercolor painting lessons at the nearby community college.

Ken has also been involved in genealogical research that began in 1973 as a result of reading a magazine article. He published a book on his mother's family four years later and then another one that focused on his father's side of the family in 2000. Today, he continues his search for the "dead limbs" that make up his family tree.

Ken's interest in gourd art began nine years ago. While enrolled in a computer class, a fellow student mentioned he was also taking a gourd decorating class. Ken's main interest with gourds is woodburning, cut-out designs, and melted crayon decoration.

JoAnne Phelps

JoAnne is a native Marylander currently living in the Jarrettsville area of Harford County. Starting at an early age, she loved creating things using anything available to her, from household goods to nature-found items.

JoAnne is self-taught in many of the arts and crafts. She now strives to increase her skills through local classes and workshops. Her goal is to try as many different arts as she can come across in the hopes of determining more specifically just what her niche might be in her retirement years. So far, JoAnne has learned paper crafting, stained glass, fused glass, toll-painting, wire sculpture, clay modeling, mosaics, jewelry making, digital imagery, macramé and other yarning methods, and various wood-working techniques, such as scroll-work, wood-turning, and woodcarving both relief and chain-saw, just to name a few. Her future sights are on glass blowing and heavier metal sculpture, but those are on hold for now as she found a fabulous new medium — "our beloved gourds" —which allows her to strengthen and combine many techniques, including wood-burning, carving, painting, and 3-D applications.

Jayne Wright

After a long wait, Jayne's schedule and a local gourd class finally meshed; thus started a love of gourds and gourding (and constant purchases of new gourd supplies). Jayne, along with her husband and daughter, recently moved to the country and acquired a big red barn with a workshop. The new space allows her to work with gourds, garden, and raise chickens. In her spare time, Jayne is a consultant in early childhood education.

Susan M. Zanella

Susan lives in Baldwin, which is on the northeast side of Maryland, about ten miles south of the Pennsylvania line and thirty miles north of Baltimore. She holds a bachelor's degree in Fine Art from the College of Notre Dame of Maryland. Susan has always loved drawing and painting in acrylics and oils, but had gotten away from any artistic endeavors since starting her own print-brokering business in 1995.

Susan first became interested in gourds after taking a computer web design class in 2005. One portion of the class was Photoshop, and the instructor used a picture of one of her gourds to demonstrate some Photoshop techniques. This led to a discussion of gourds during a break in class, which led Susan to sign up for a gourd class that was taught by the same instructor. The first gourd class was centered on learning that a hard-shell gourd has many of the same properties as soft wood and some of what can be done artistically with them. Susan realized not only how much she missed the creative process, but also how much of her spirit was lost in not pursuing any creative outlet. The variations of creativity that can be done with a gourd are only limited to a person's imagination.

Susan has found that hard-shell gourds are an extremely unique canvas provided by nature. She loves the three-dimensionality of the canvas and tries to have her designs encompass all 360-degrees of that surface, although some projects lend themselves to only one side or another. A hard-shell gourd is not uniform to itself, as no two gourds are alike. The uniqueness of its surface will sometimes lend itself to the design she has envisioned, but sometimes the patterns are what create the vision of the design itself. Susan says that she loves the surprises her gourd canvas reveals to her and the variation her projects take on because of the unpredictability of the canvas.

Resources

This is not a complete list of gourd suppliers.
This is a list of suppliers that I use for most of my supplies.

Raw Gourd Suppliers

Beiler's Gourds
Lancaster, Pennsylvania
717-687-8797

Pumpkin Hollow
Piggott, Arkansas
870-598-3568
www.pumpkinhollow.com

Smucker's Gourd Farm
Kinzer, Pennsylvania
717-354-6118

Welburn Gourd Farm
Fallbrook, California
877-420-2613
www.welburngourdfarm.com

Wuertz Gourds
Casa Grande, Arizona
520-723-4432
www.wuertzfarm.com

Gourd Supplies

Arizona Gourds
Tucson, Arizona
www.arizonagourds.com

The Caning Shop
Berkeley, California
1-800-544-3373
www.caning.com

Craft Supplies USA
Provo, Utah
1-800-551-8876
www.woodturnerscatalog.com

Turtle Feathers
Bryson City, North Carolina
828-488-8586
www.turtlefeathers.net

Bibliography

Barnes, Marianne. *Weaving on Gourds*. Atglen, Pennsylvania: Schiffer Publishing Ltd., 2010.

Bemrose, William. *Bemrose on Traditional Woodworking: Carving, Fretwork, Buhl Work, and Marquetry*. Mineola, New York: Dover Publications, 2009.

Irish, Lora S. *101 Artistic Relief Patterns for Woodcarvers, Woodburners, & Crafters*. East Petersburg, Pennsylvania: Fox Chapel Publishing Co., Inc., 2009.

Great Book of Floral Patterns. East Petersburg, Pennsylvania: Fox Chapel Publishing Co., Inc., 2009.

Landscapes in Relief. East Petersburg, Pennsylvania: Fox Chapel Publishing Co., Inc., 2009.

Martin, Terry and Keven Wallace. *New Masters of Woodturning*. East Petersburg, Pennsylvania: Fox Chapel Publishing Co., Inc., 2008.

Mey, Sue. *Lighted Scroll Saw Projects*. Atglen, Pennsylvania: Schiffer Publishing Ltd., 2010.

Sloan, Betsey. *InLace Techniques: Resin Inlays for Gourds and Wood Crafts*. Atglen, Pennsylvania: Schiffer Publishing Ltd., 2009.

Widess, Jim and Ginger Summit. *Complete Book of Gourd Carving*. New York, New York: Sterling Publishing Co., Inc., 2004.

Gourd Pyrography. New York, New York: Sterling Publishing Co., Inc., 2002.